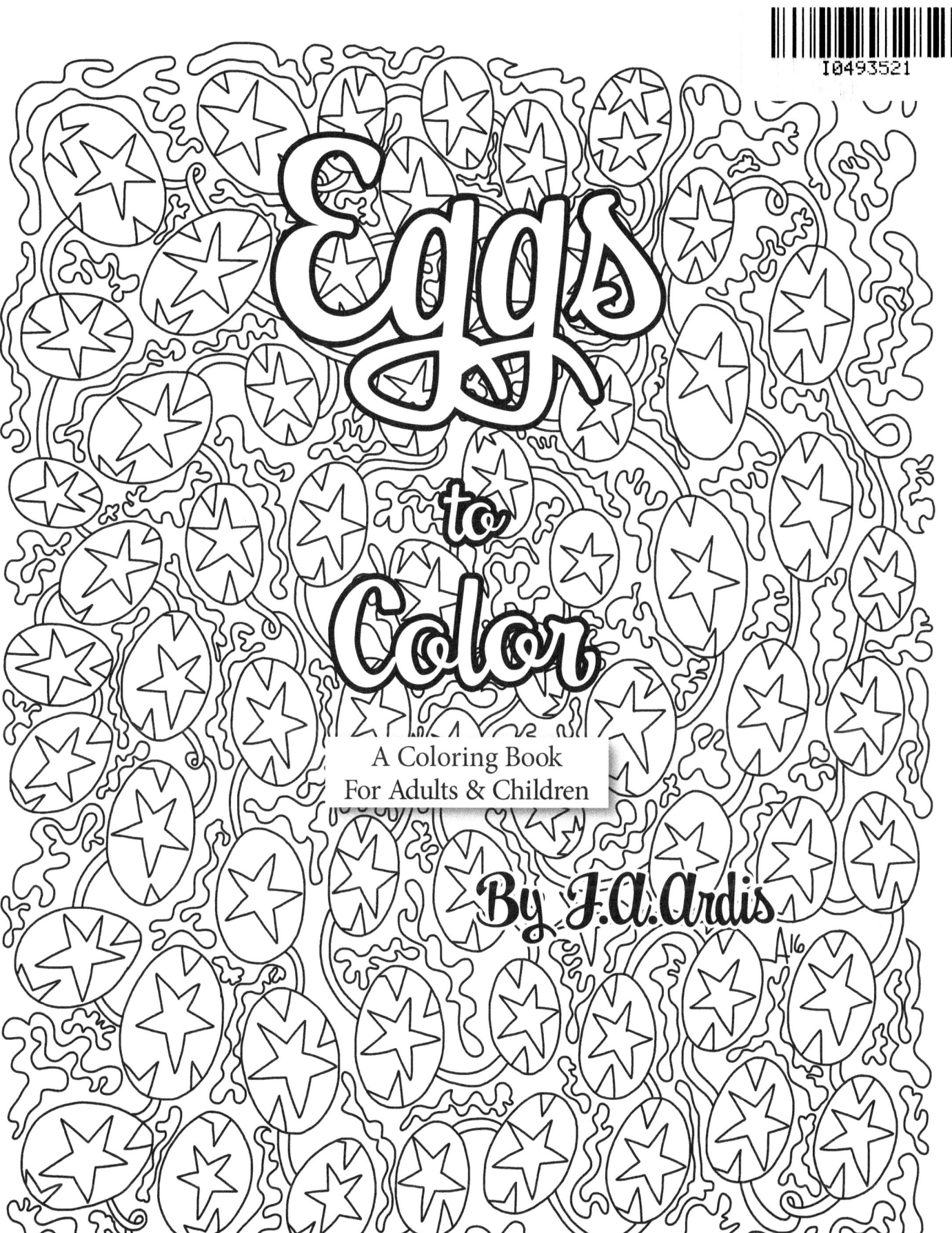

Eggs to Color

A Coloring Book For Adults & Children

By J.A. Ardis

For my mother.

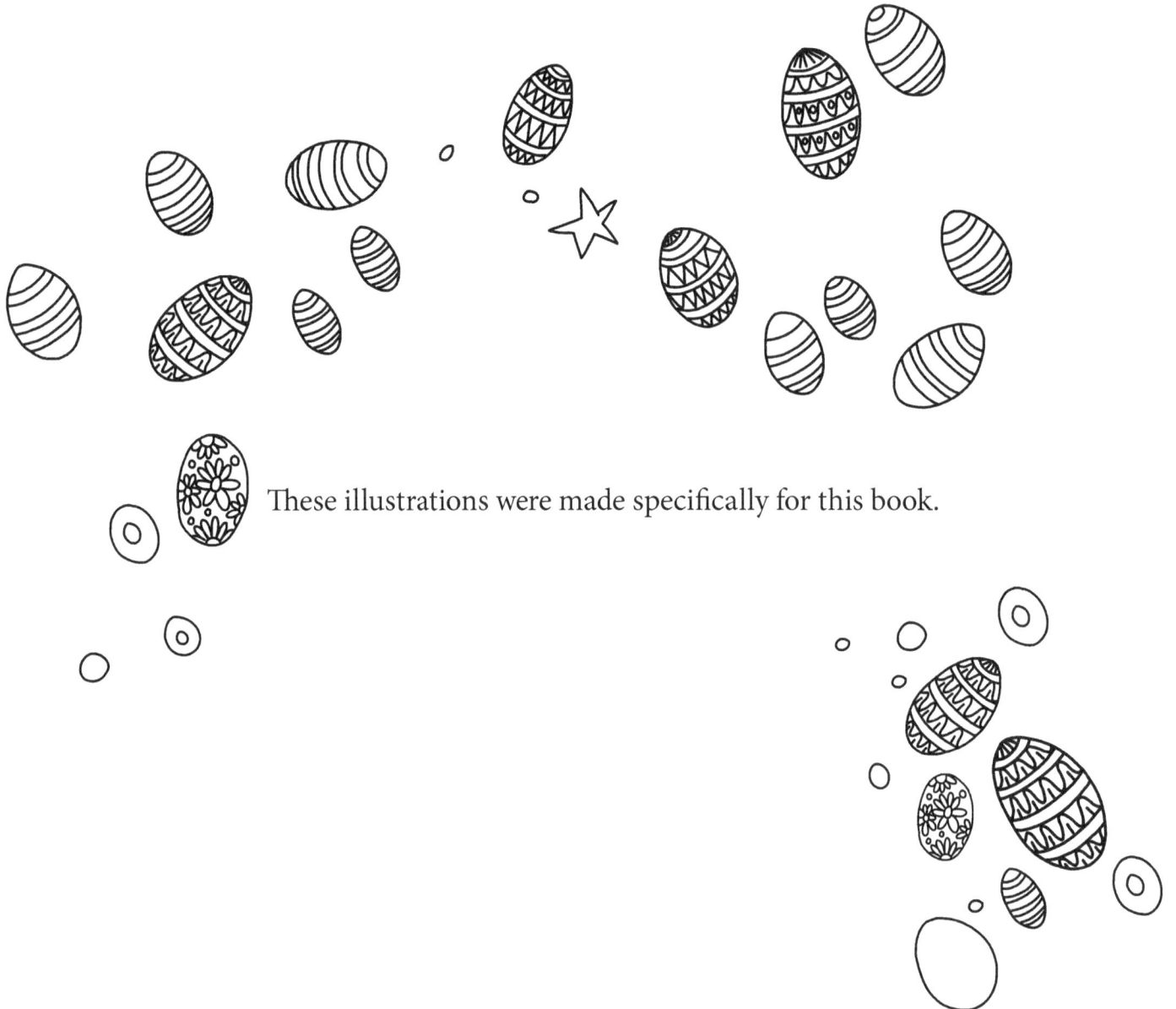

These illustrations were made specifically for this book.

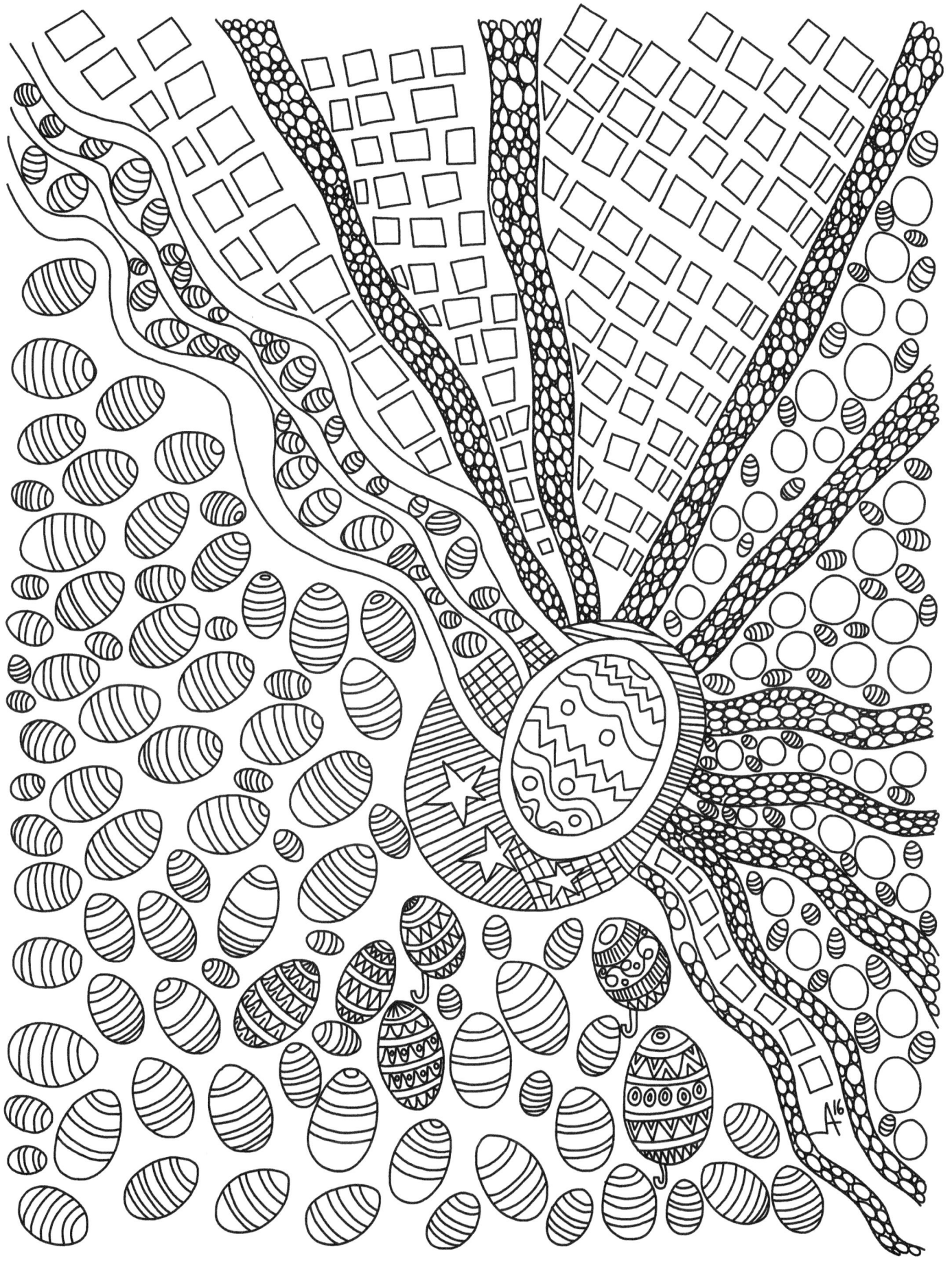

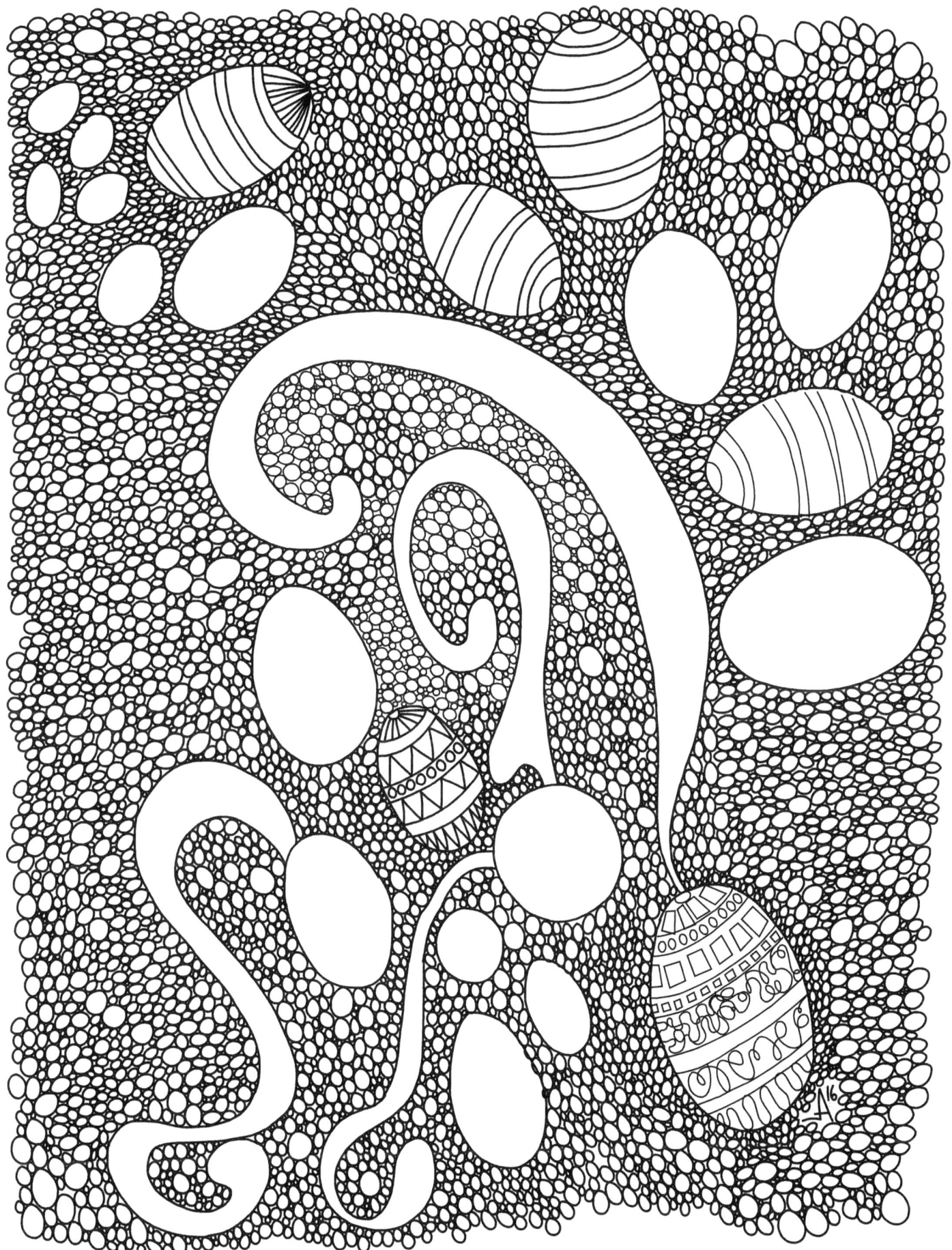

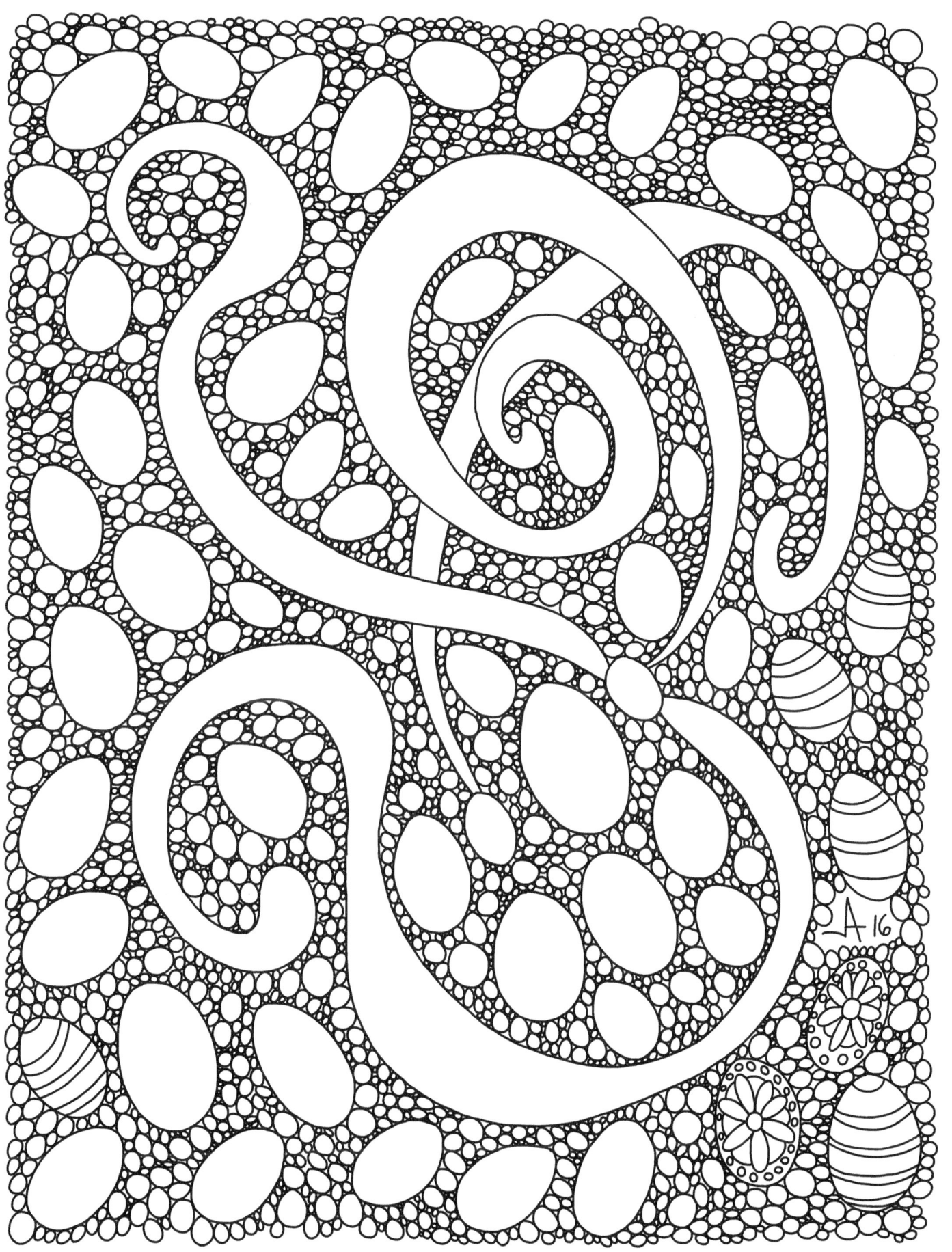

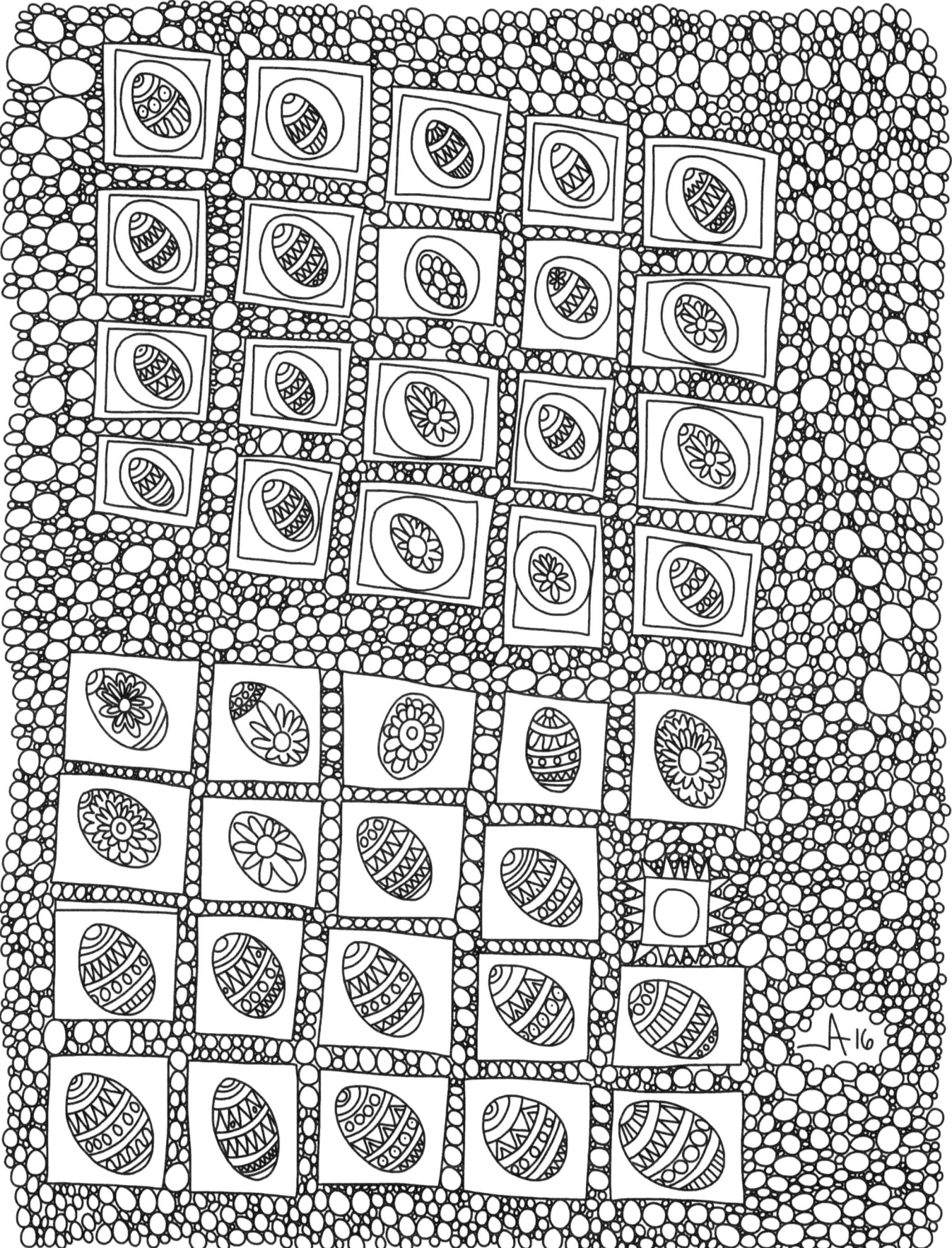

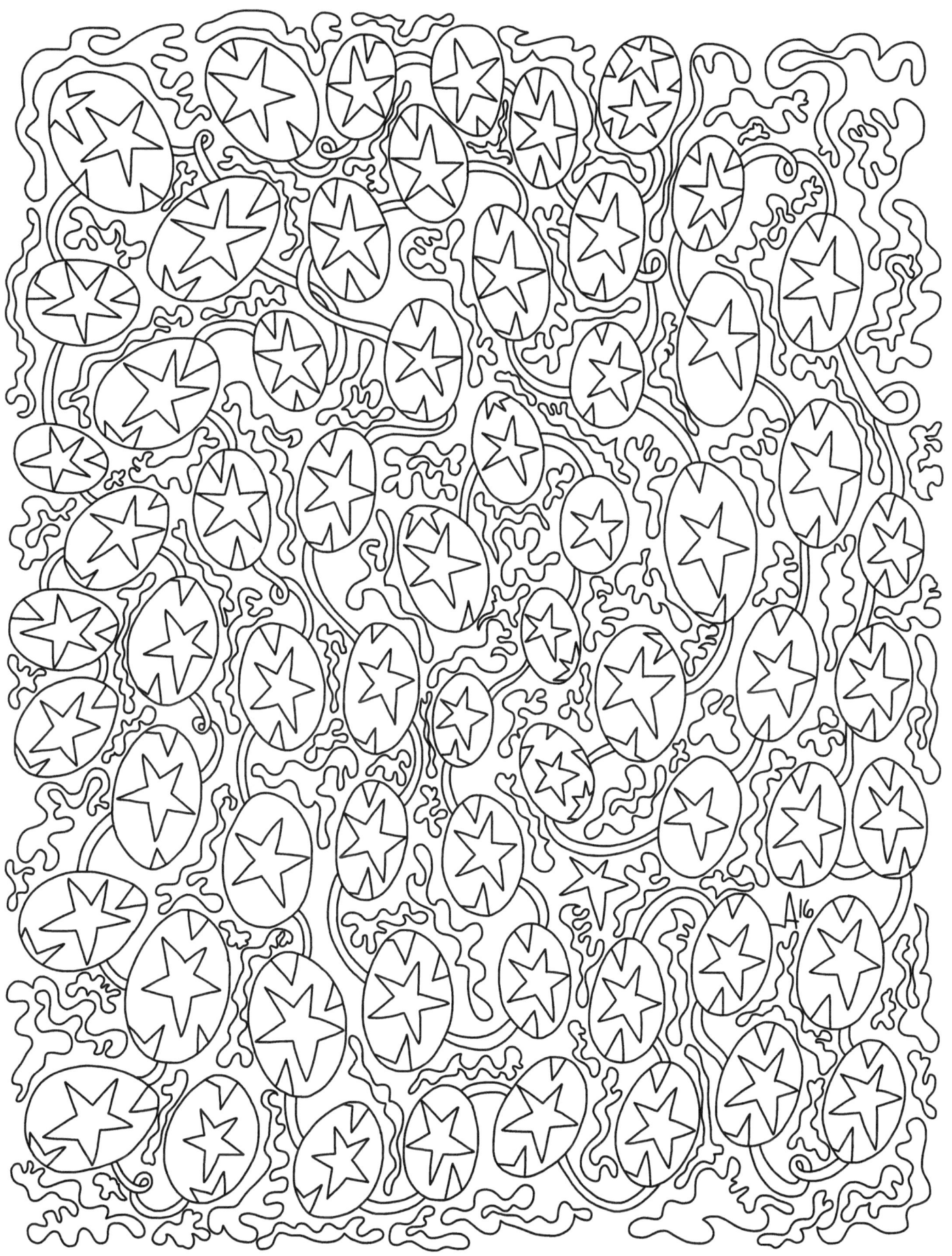

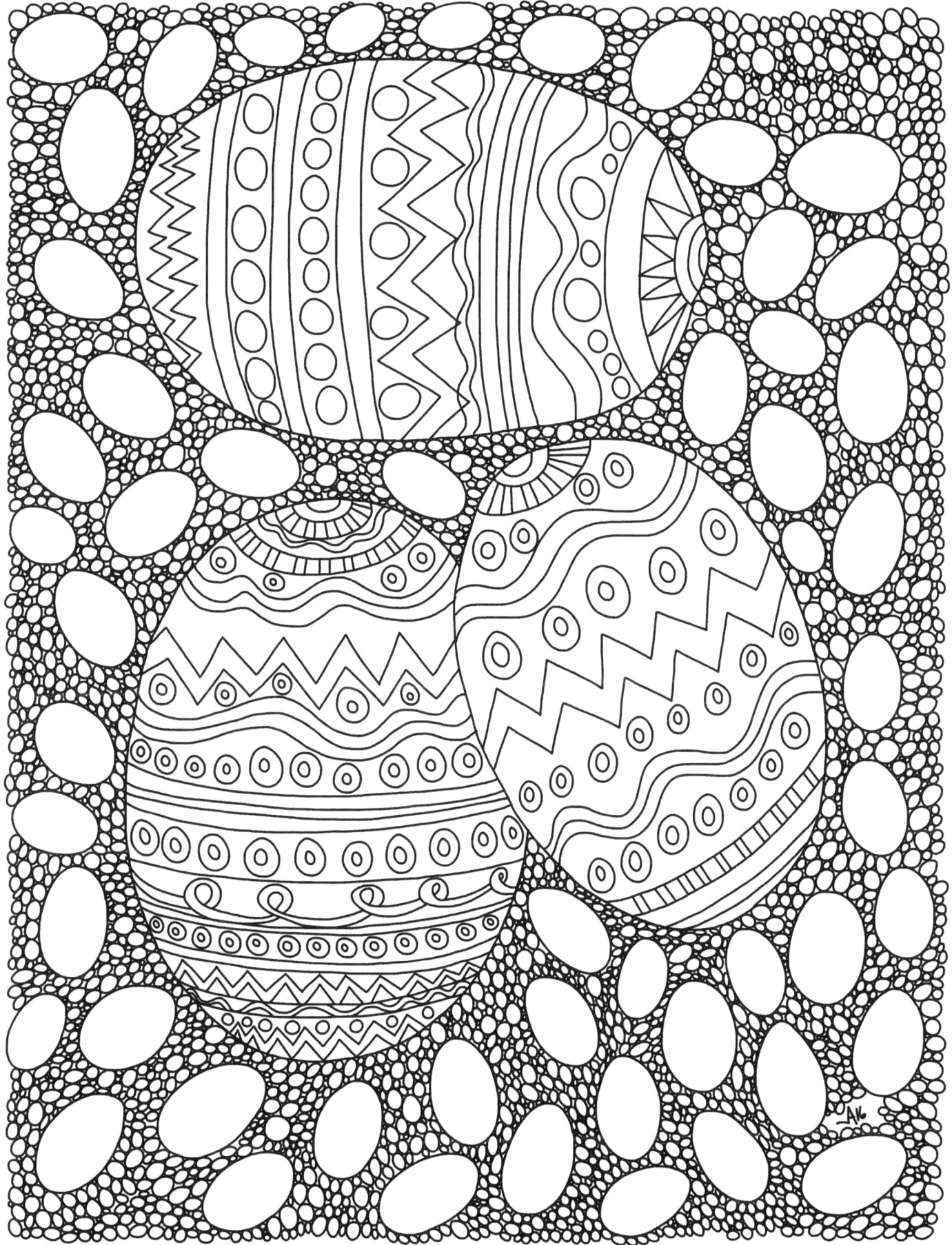

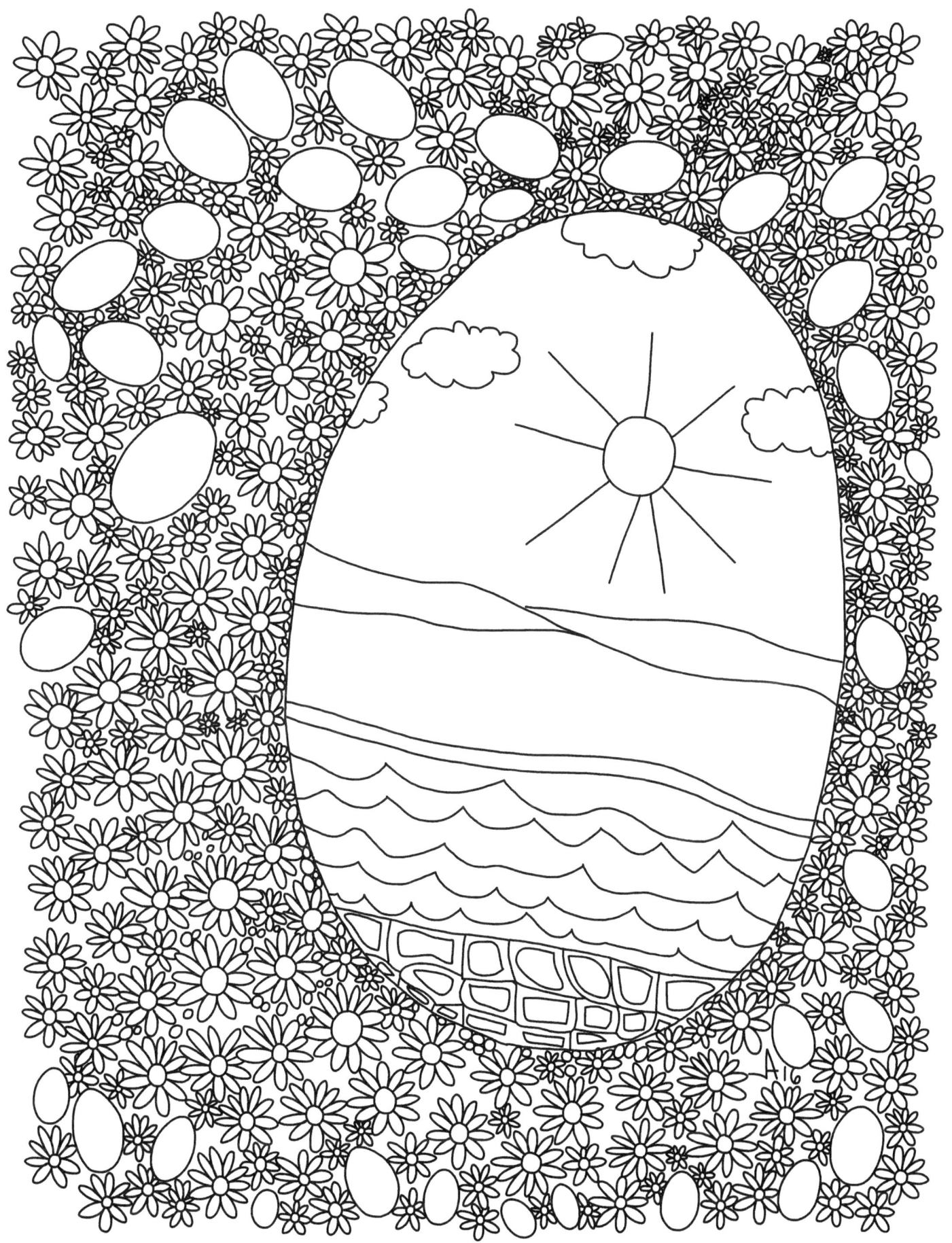

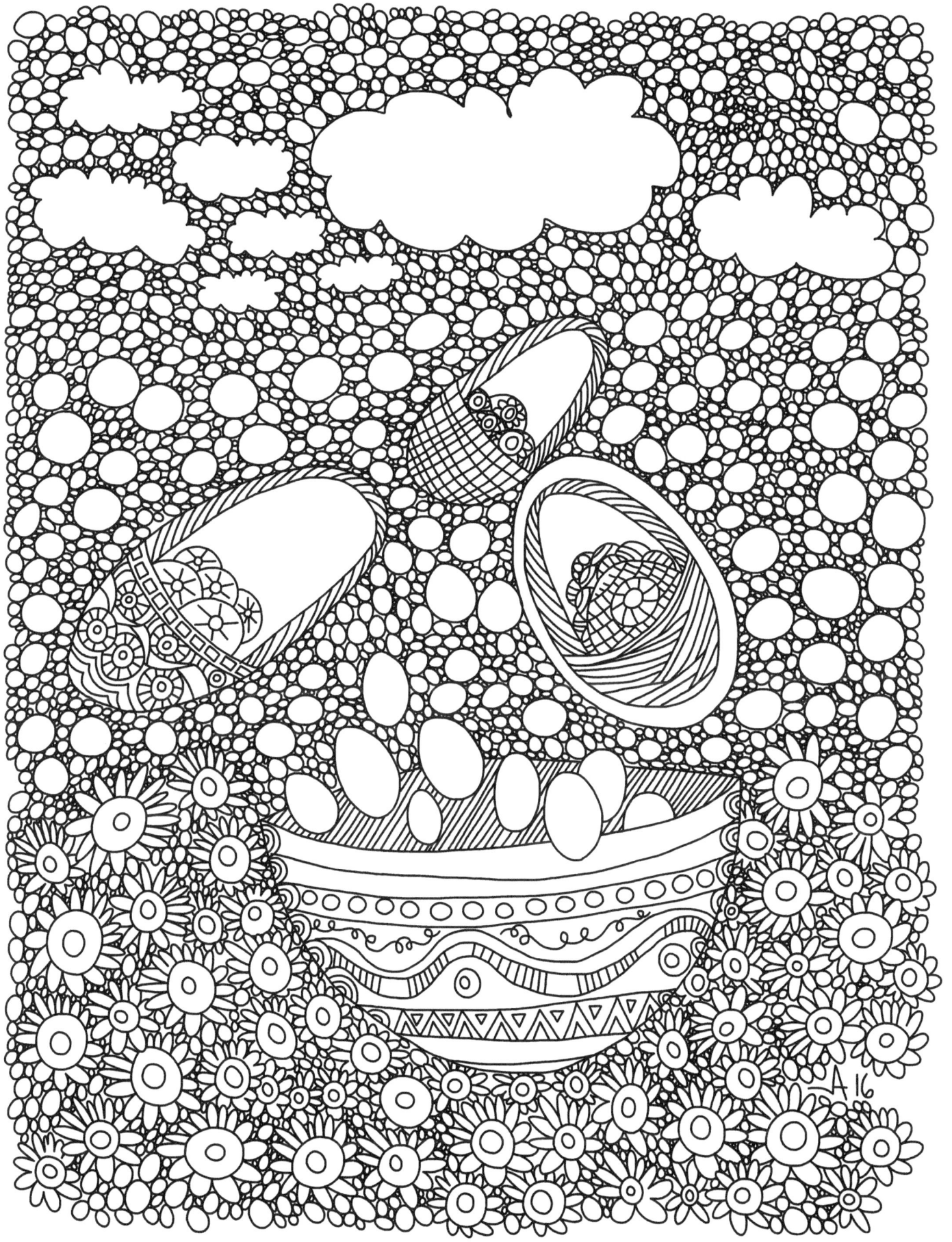

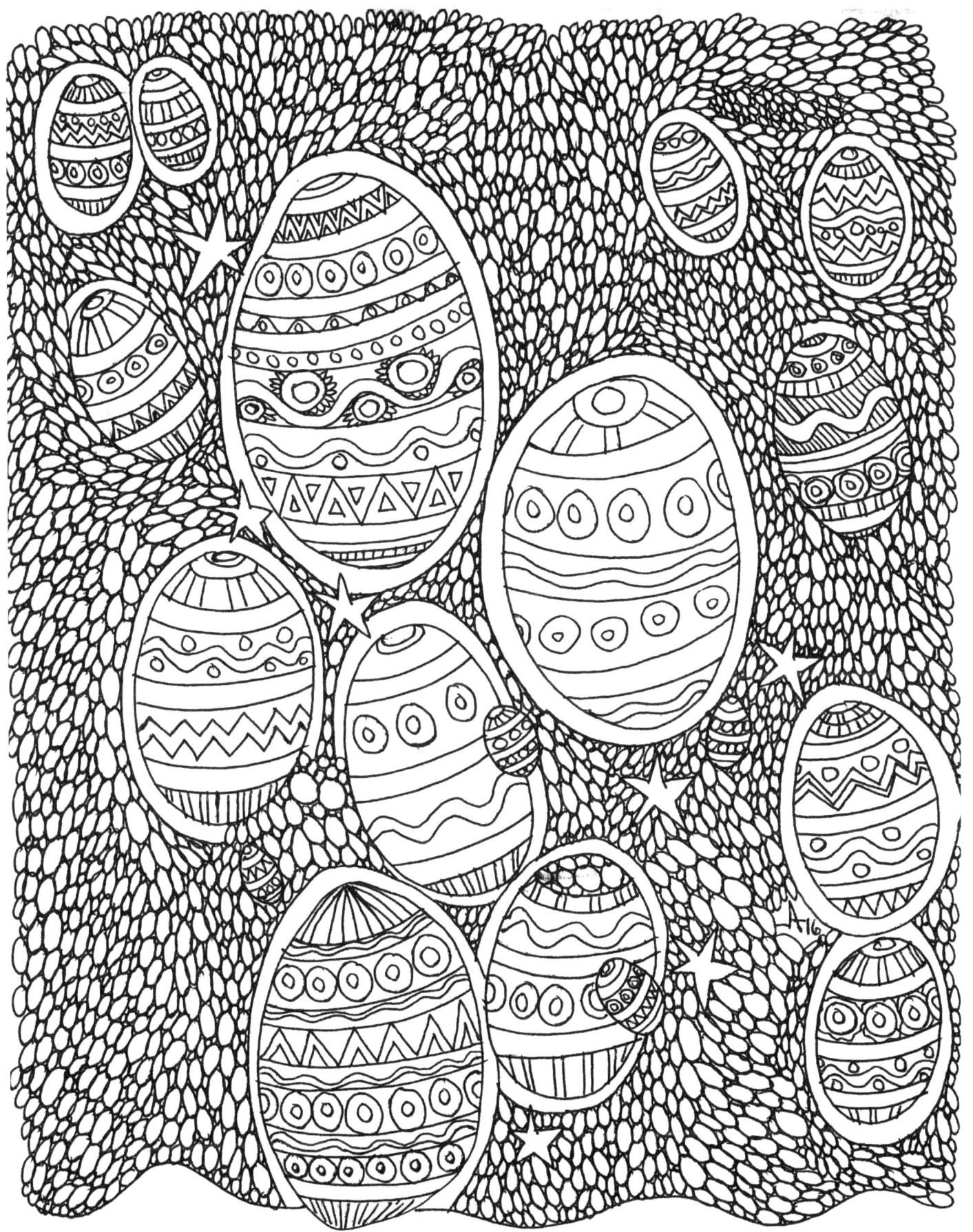

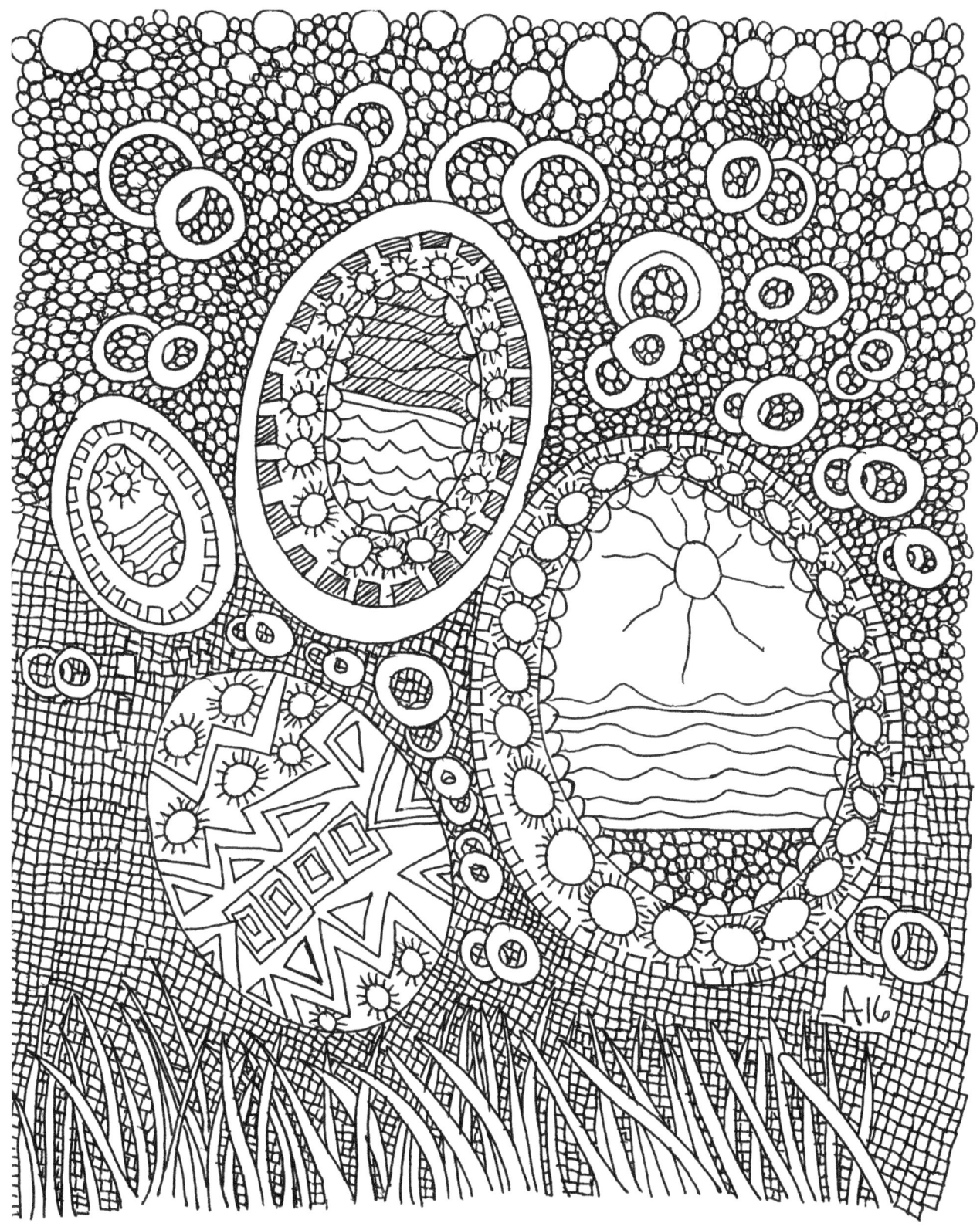

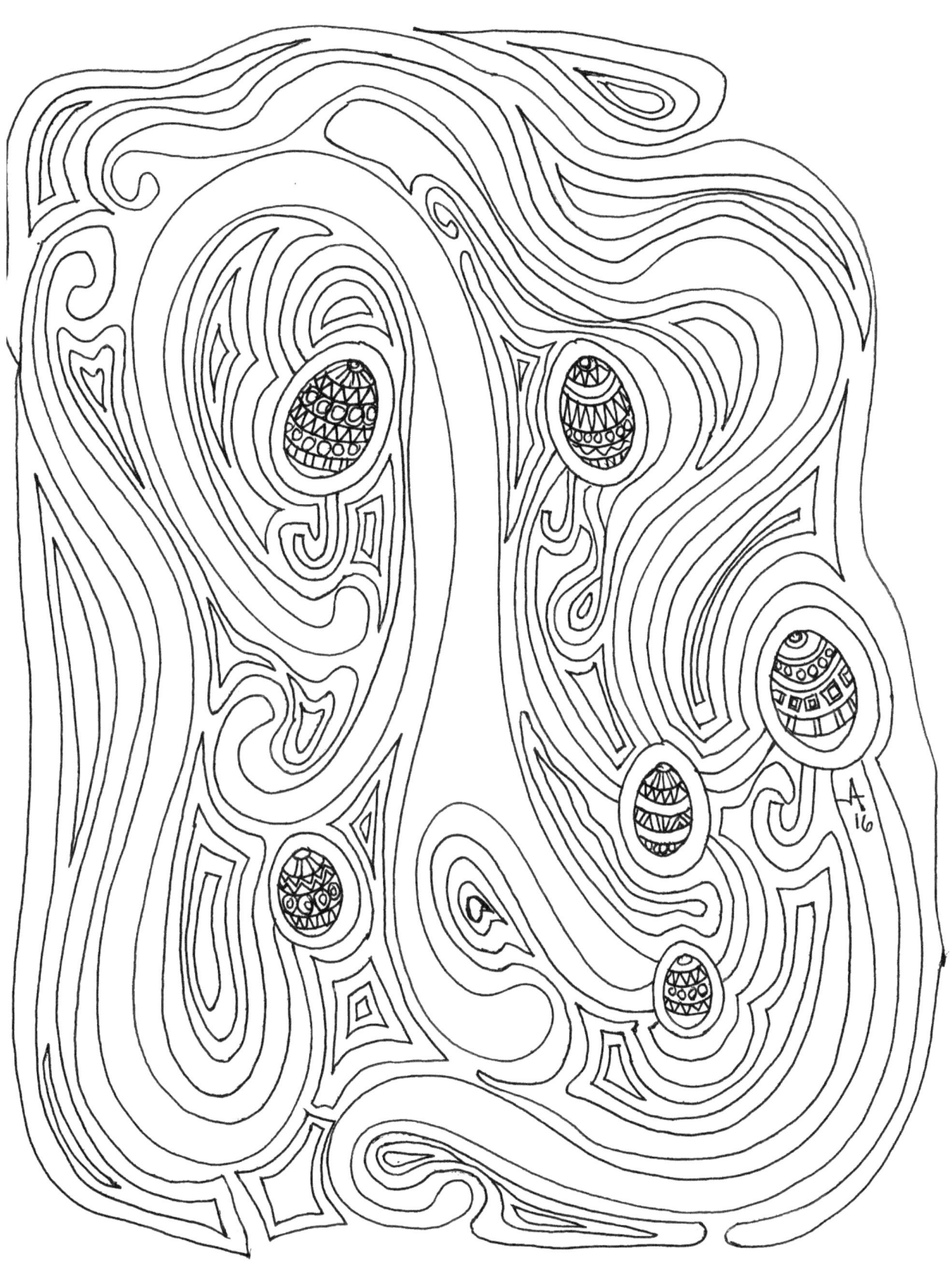

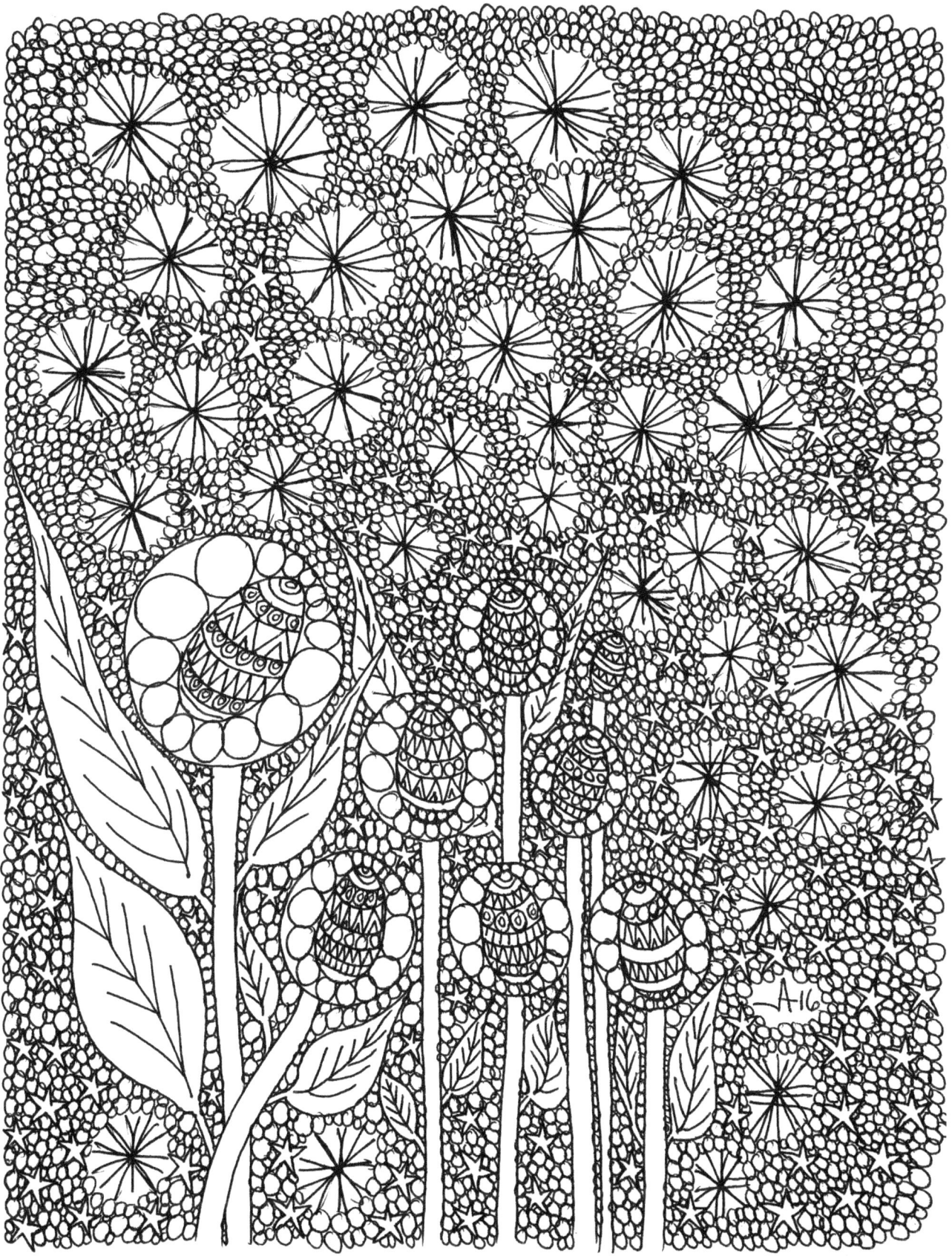

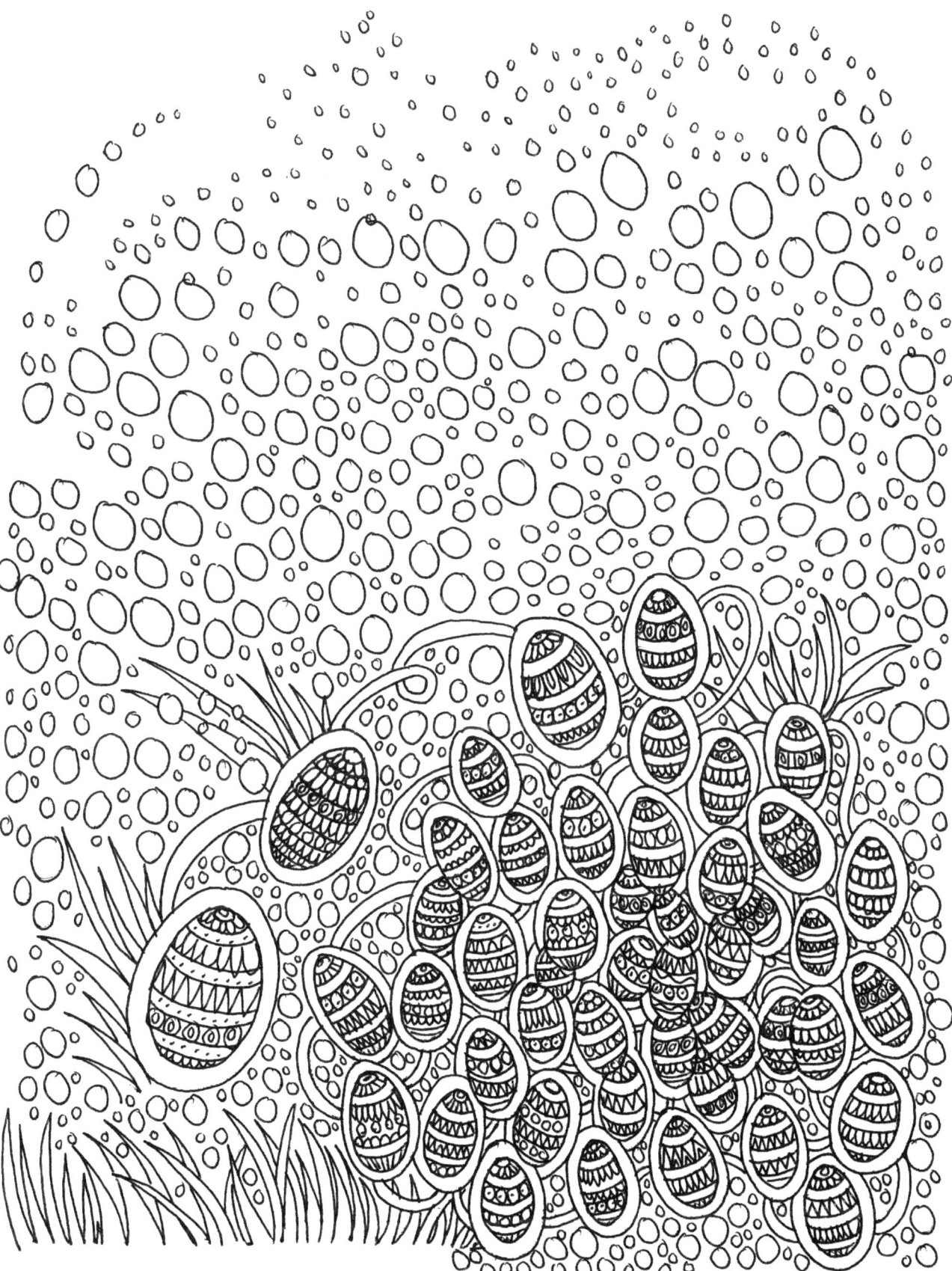

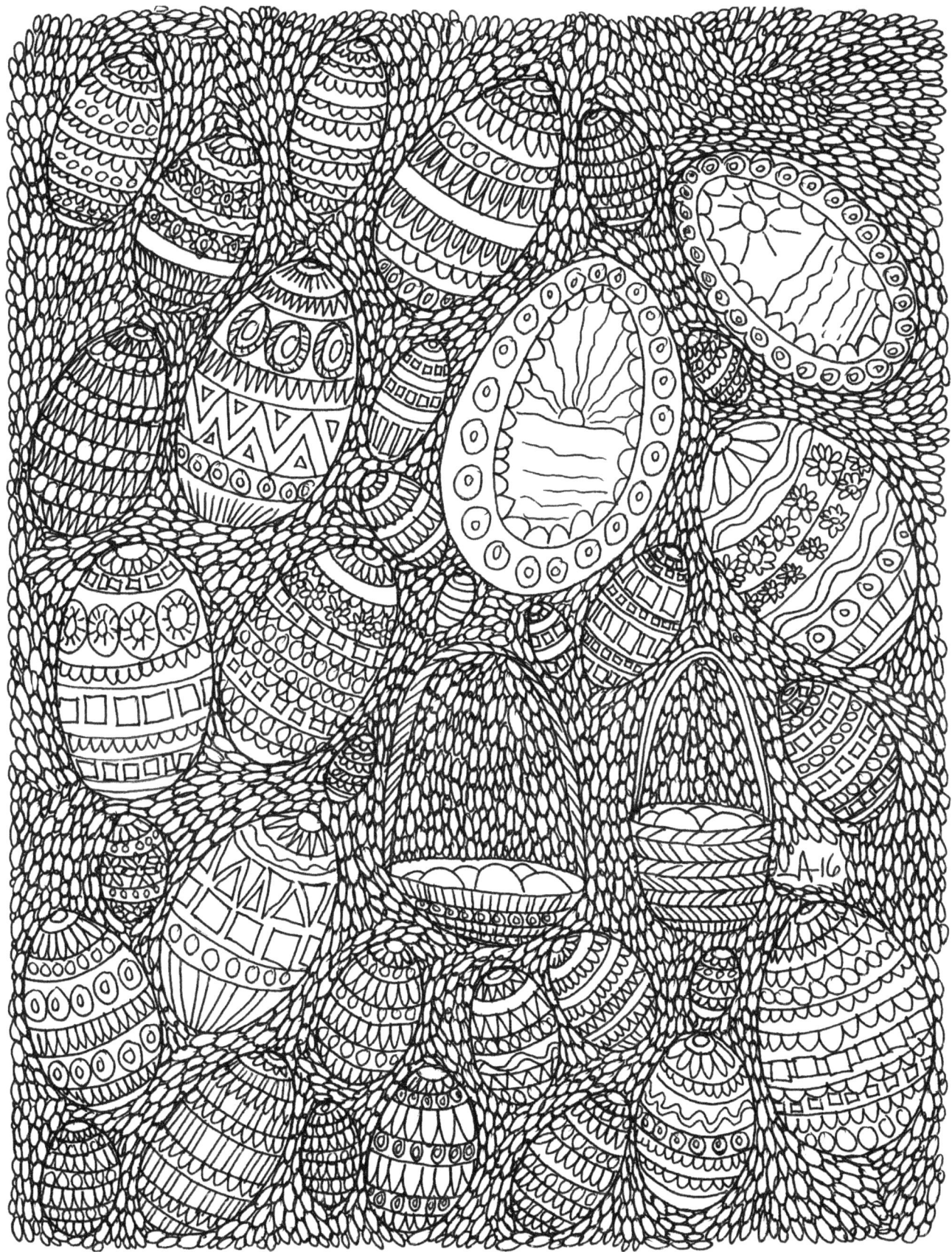

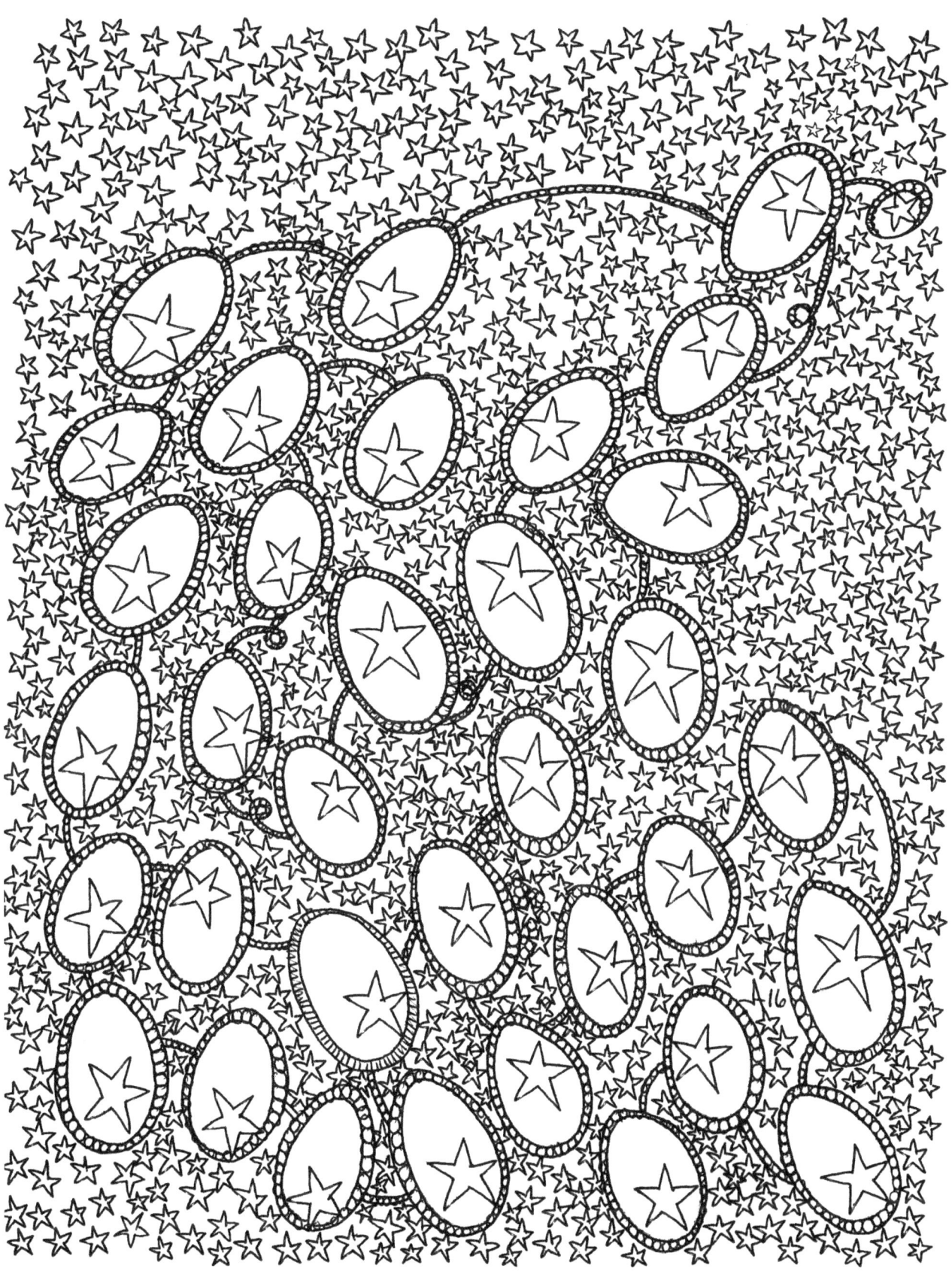

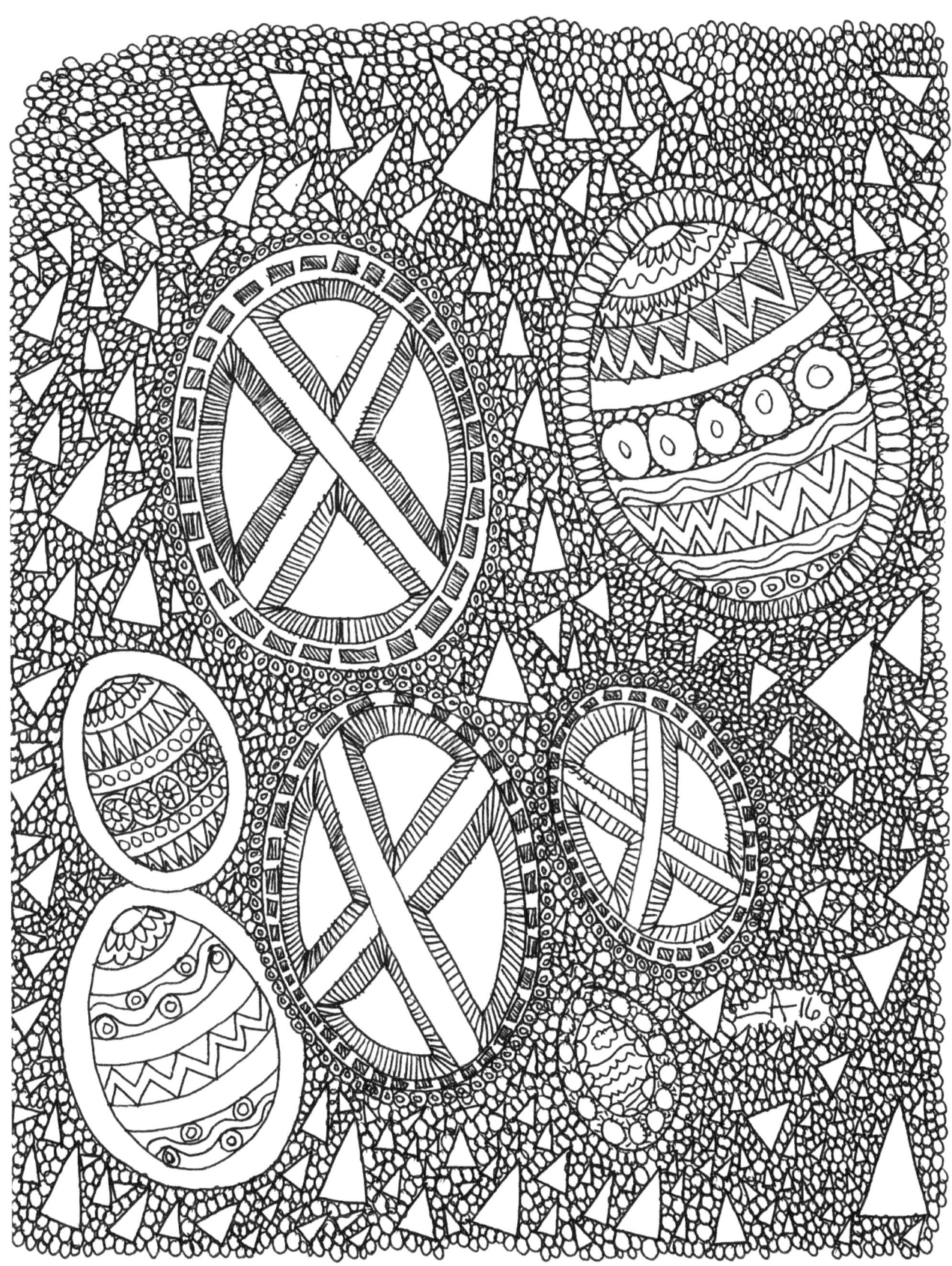

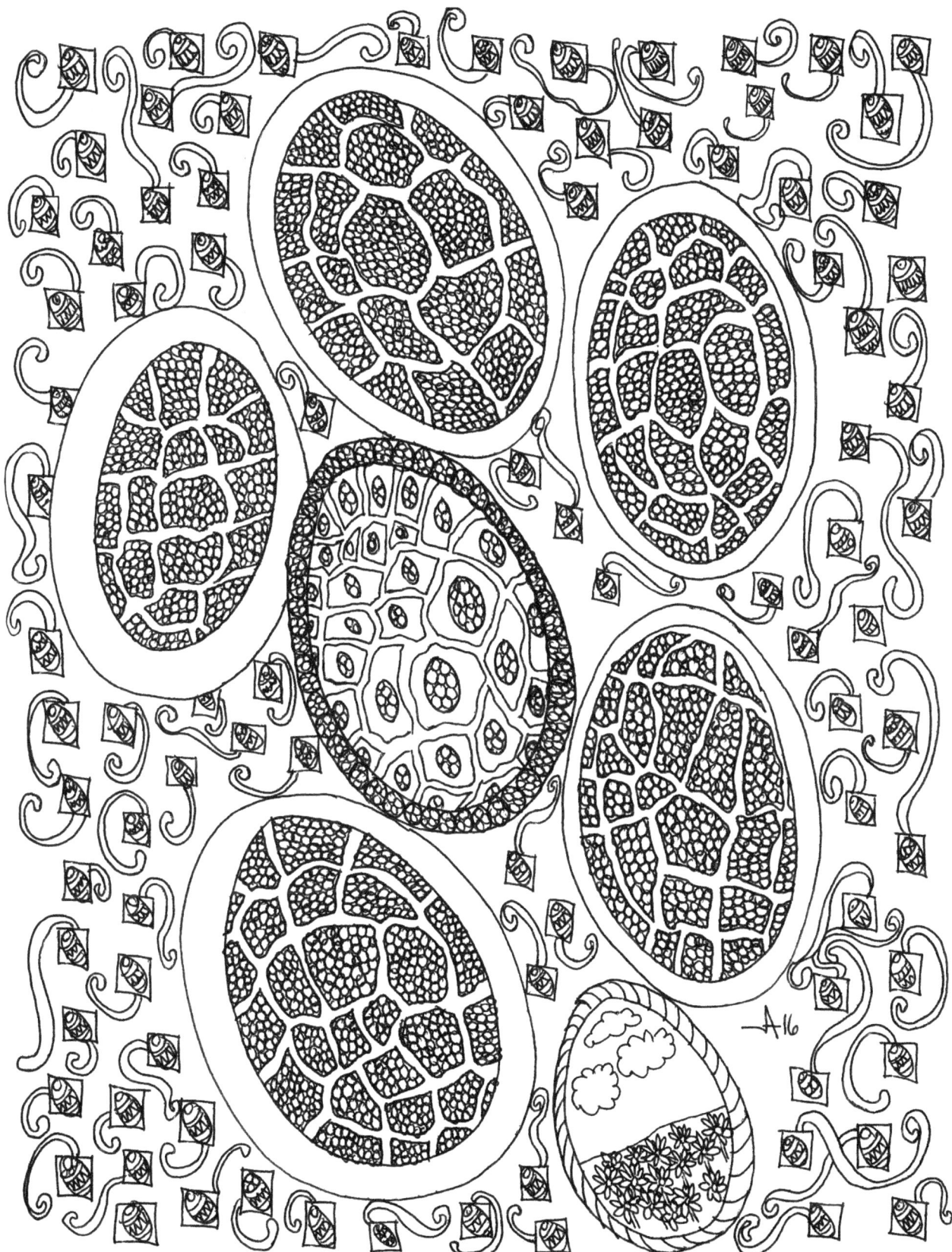

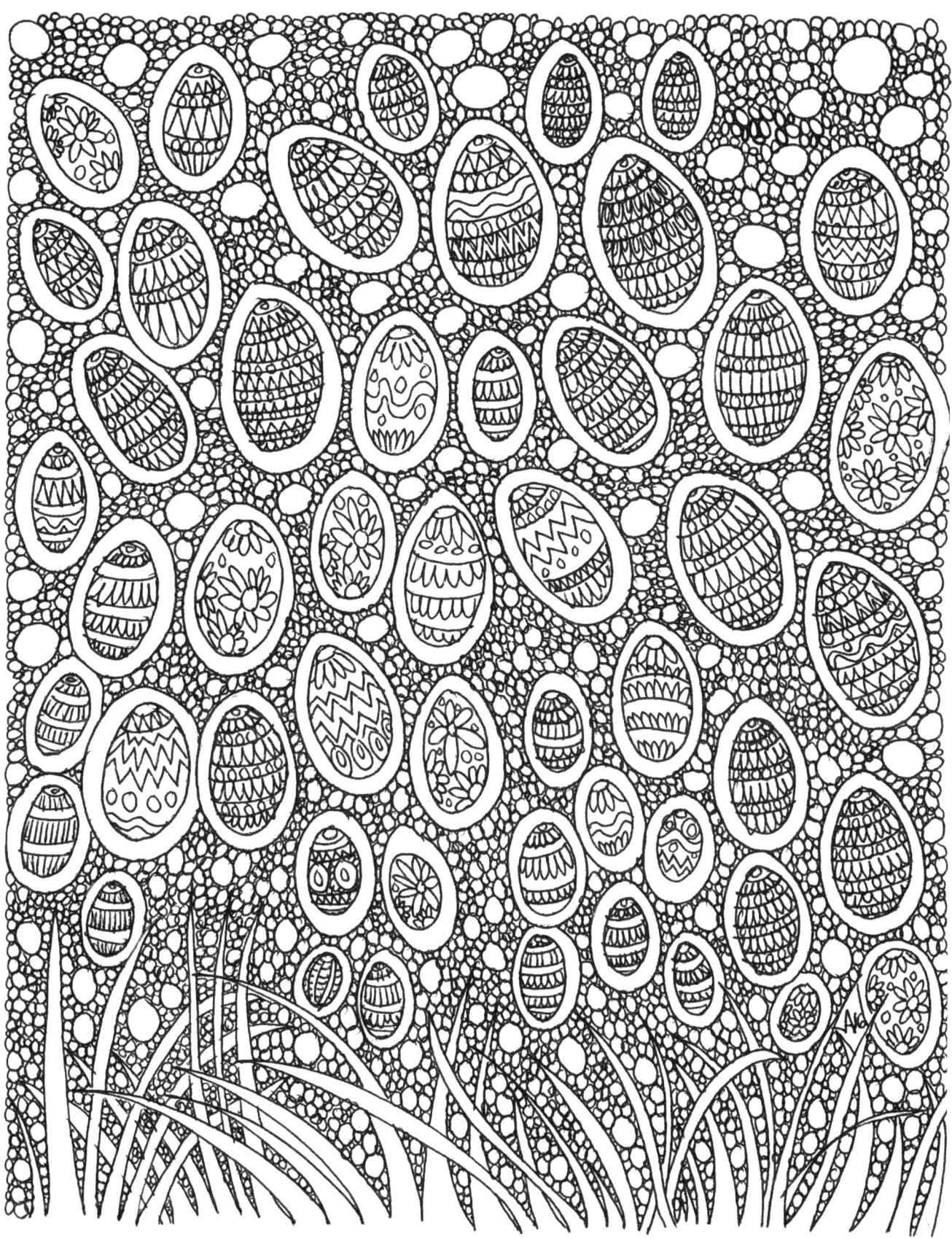

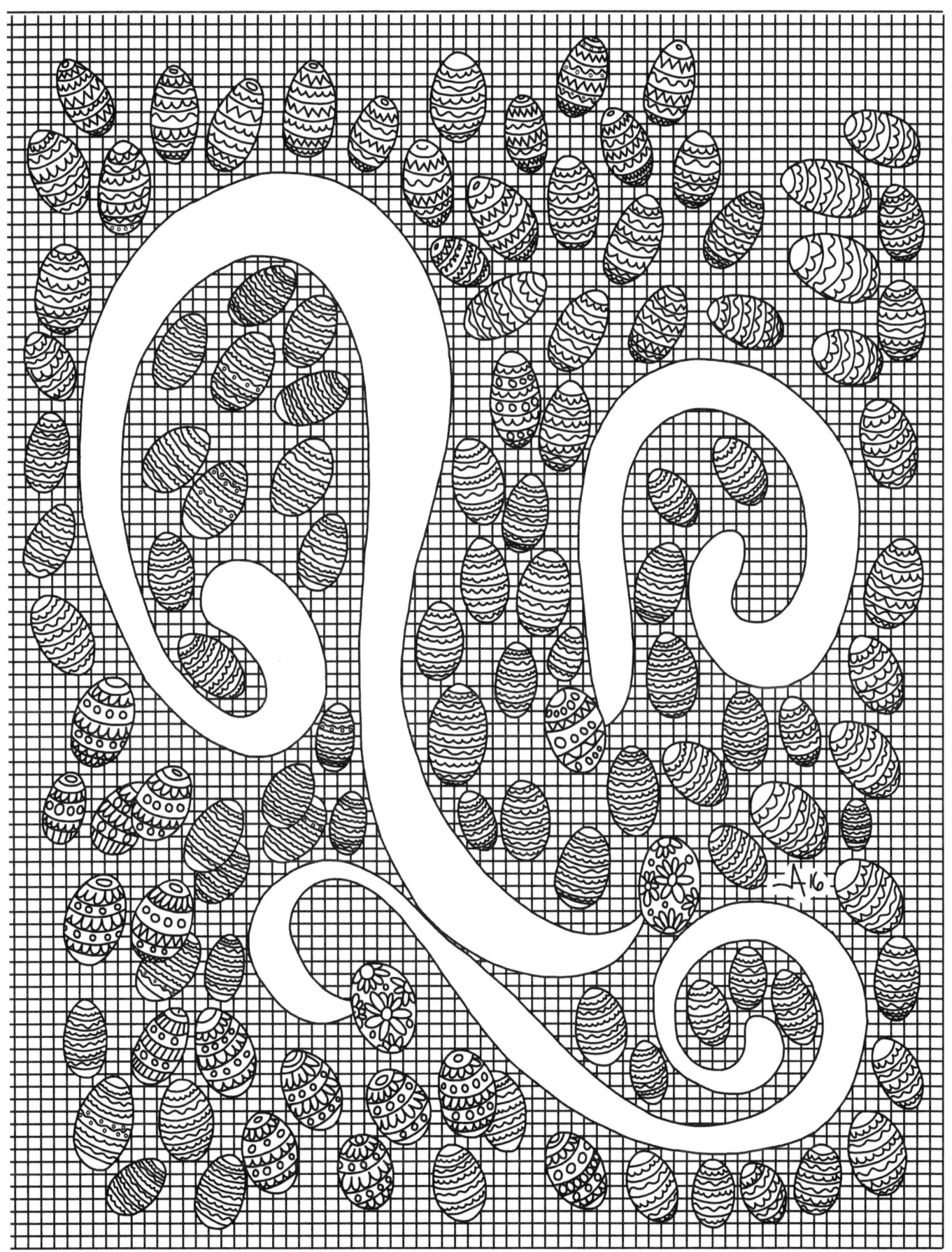

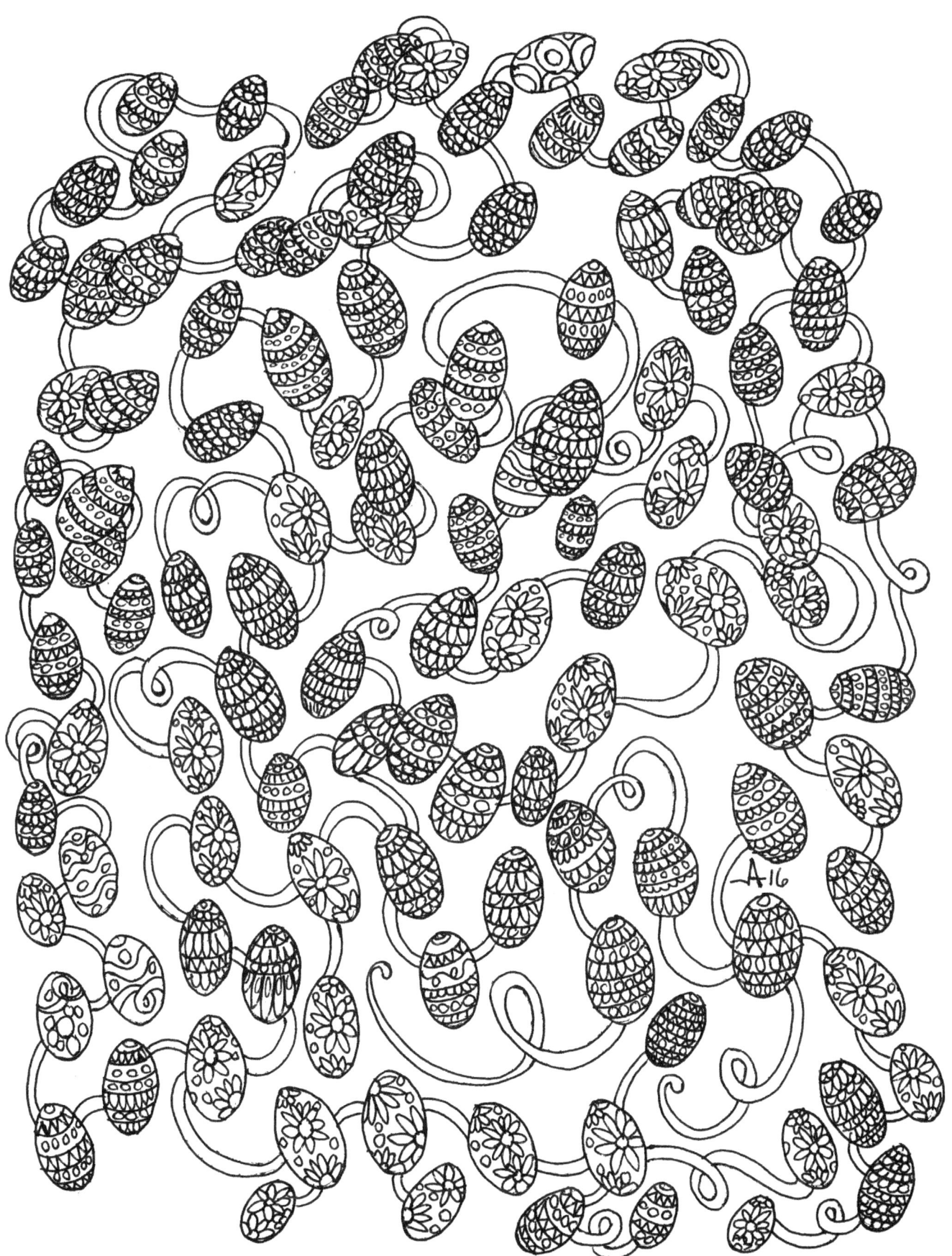

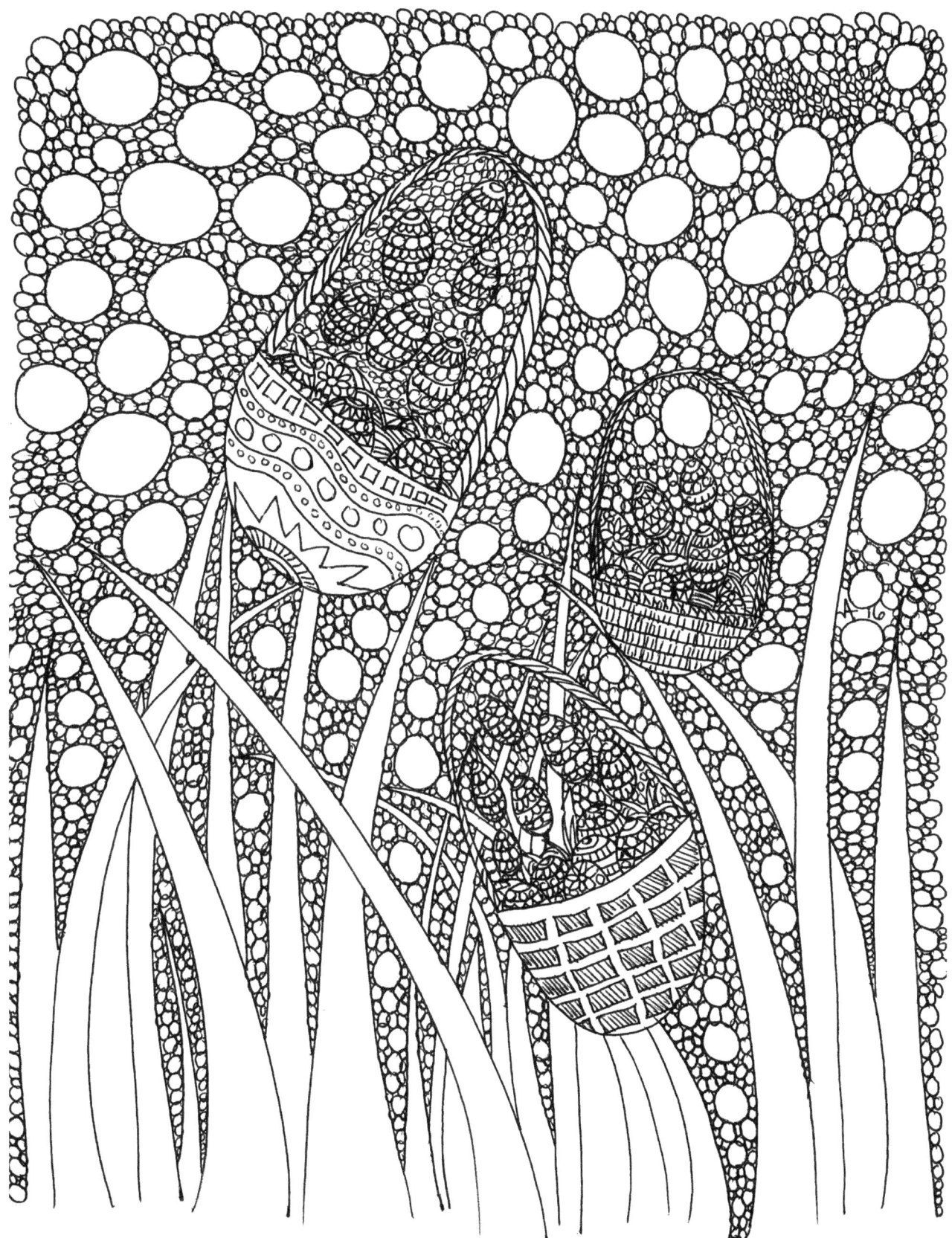

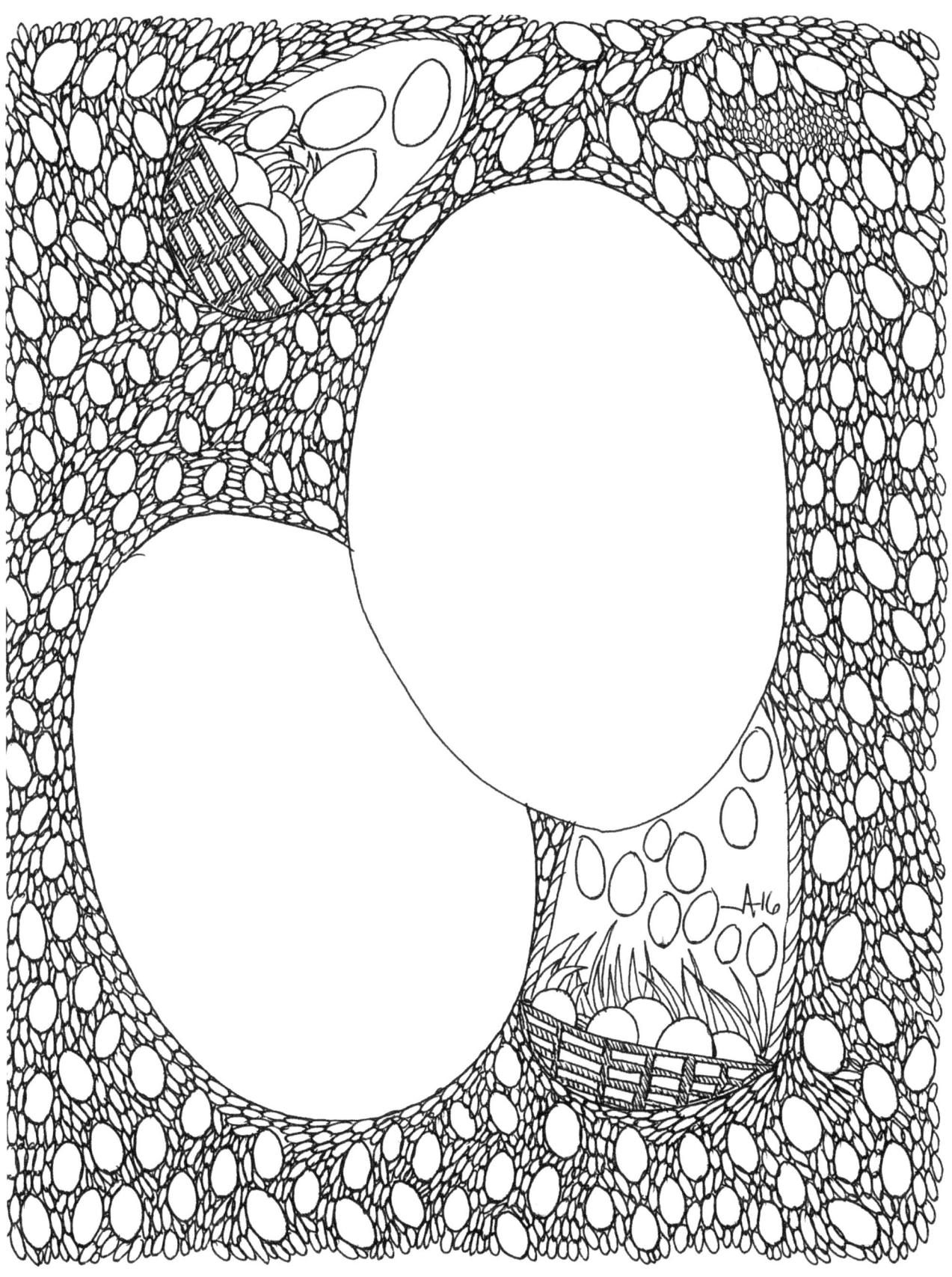

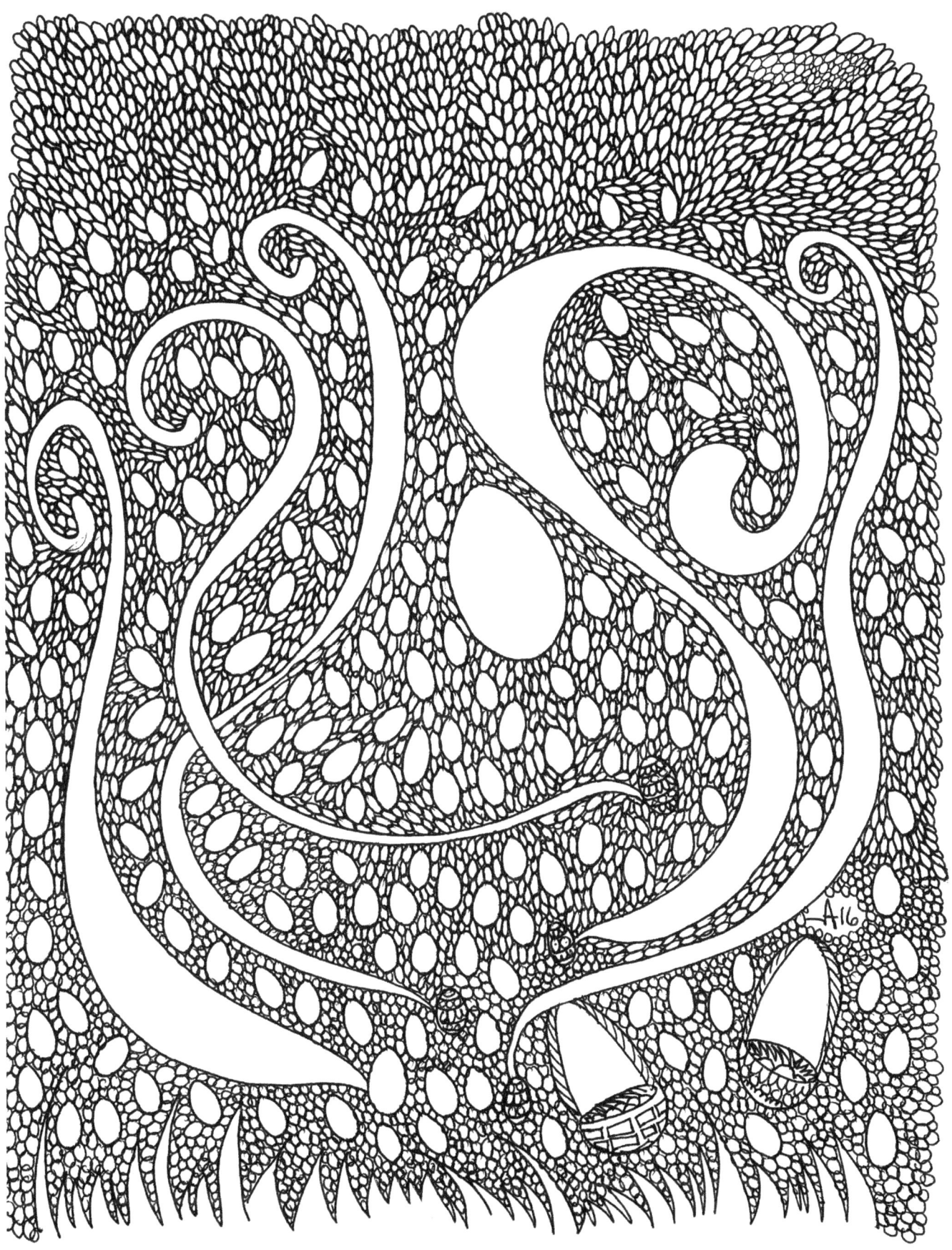

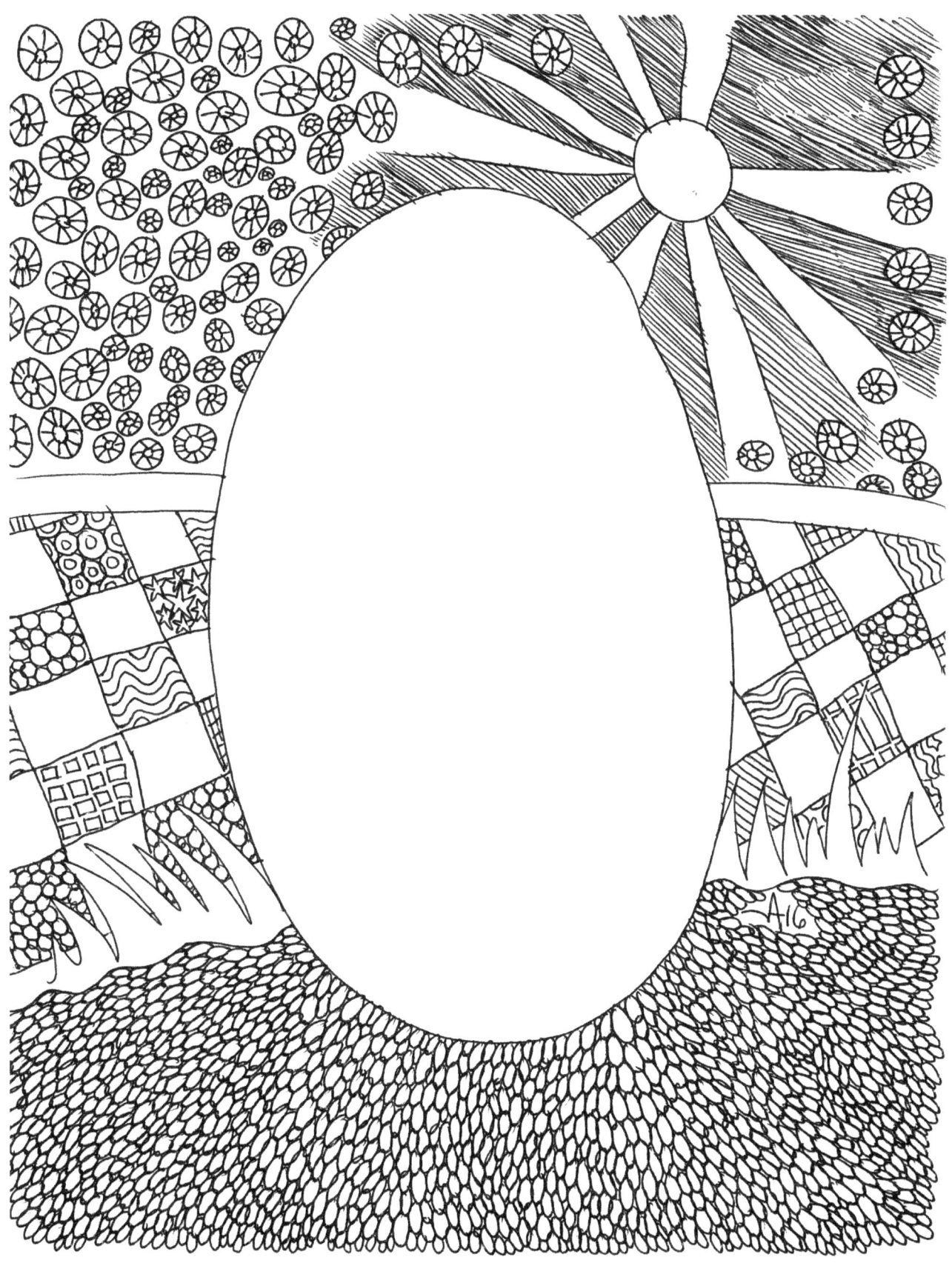

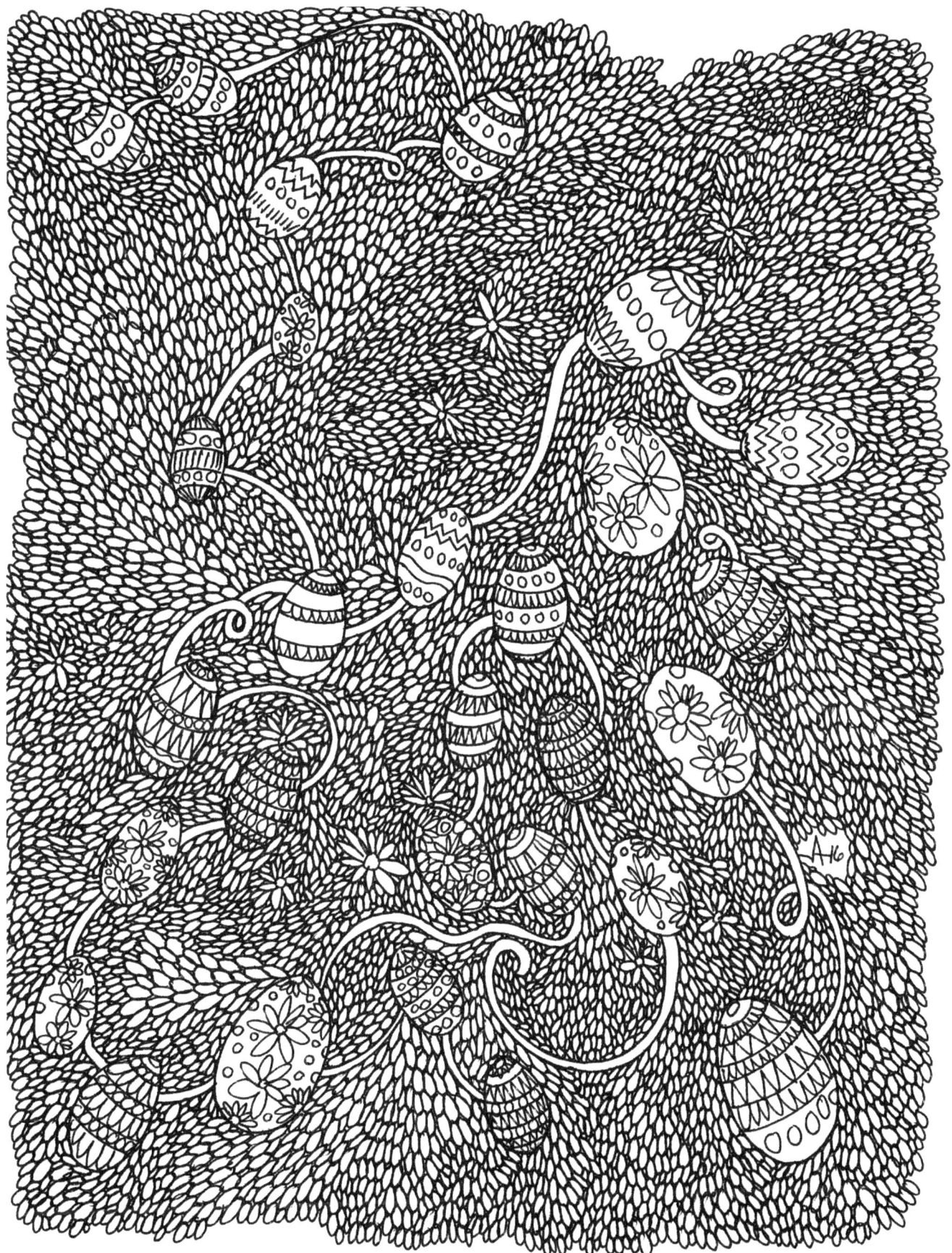

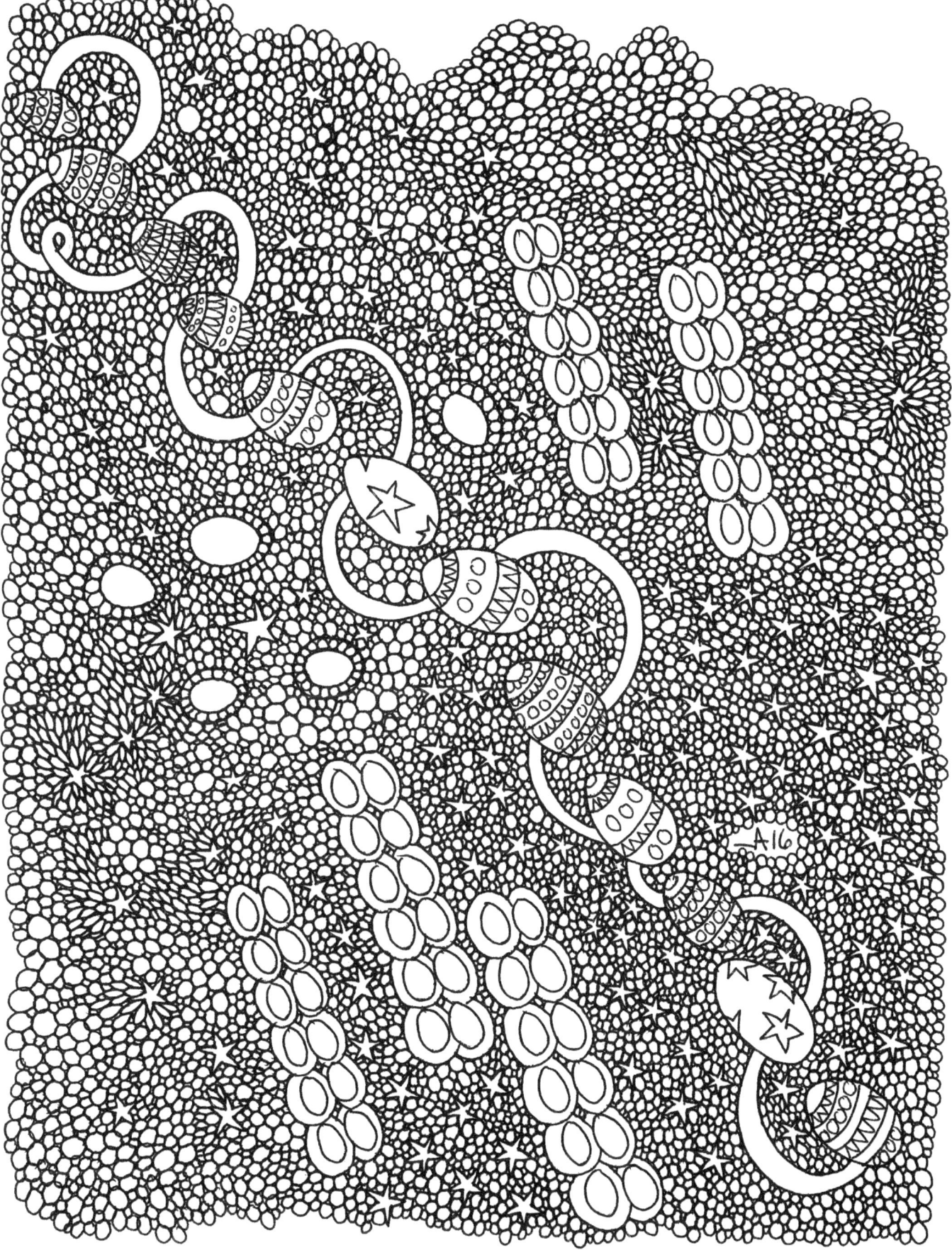

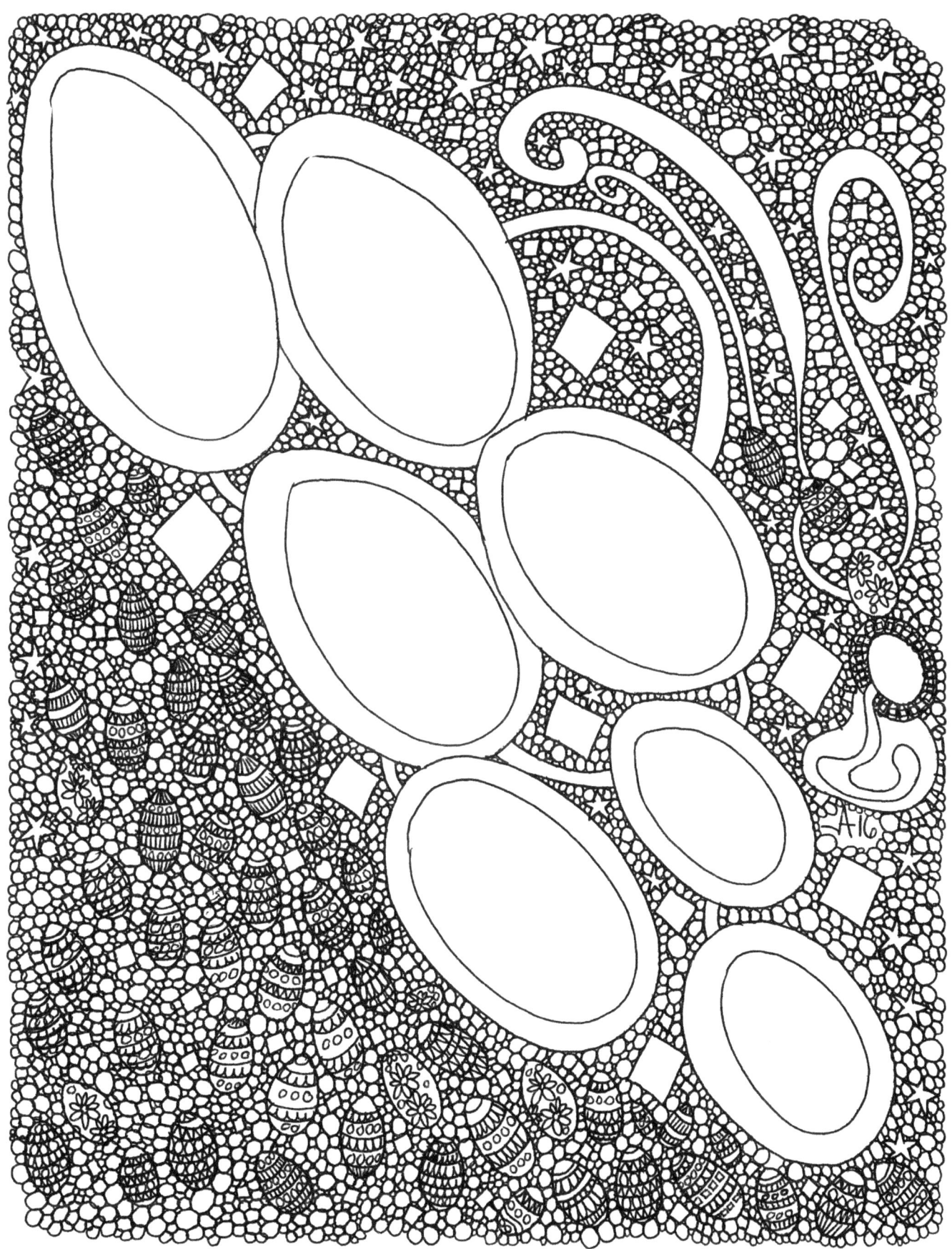

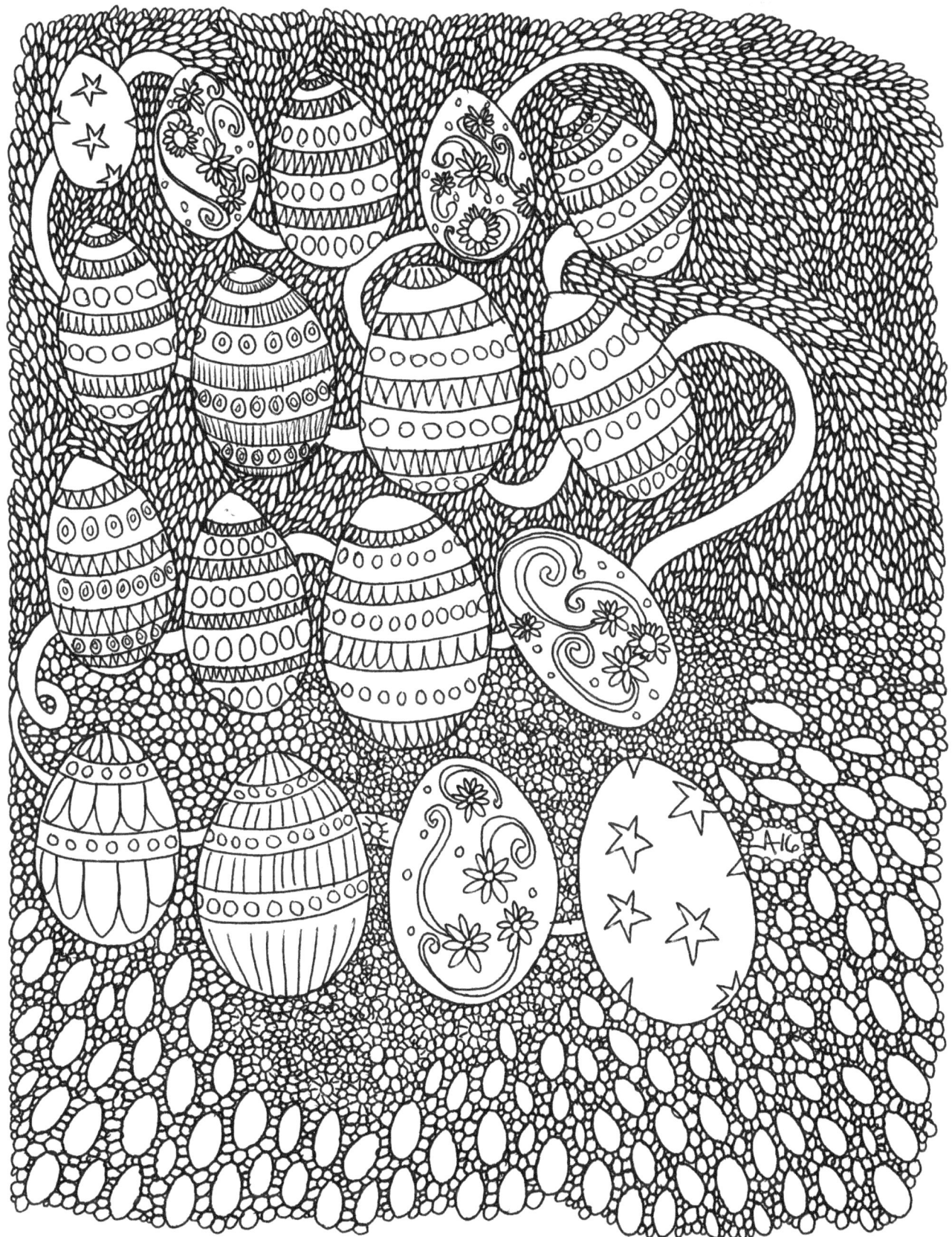

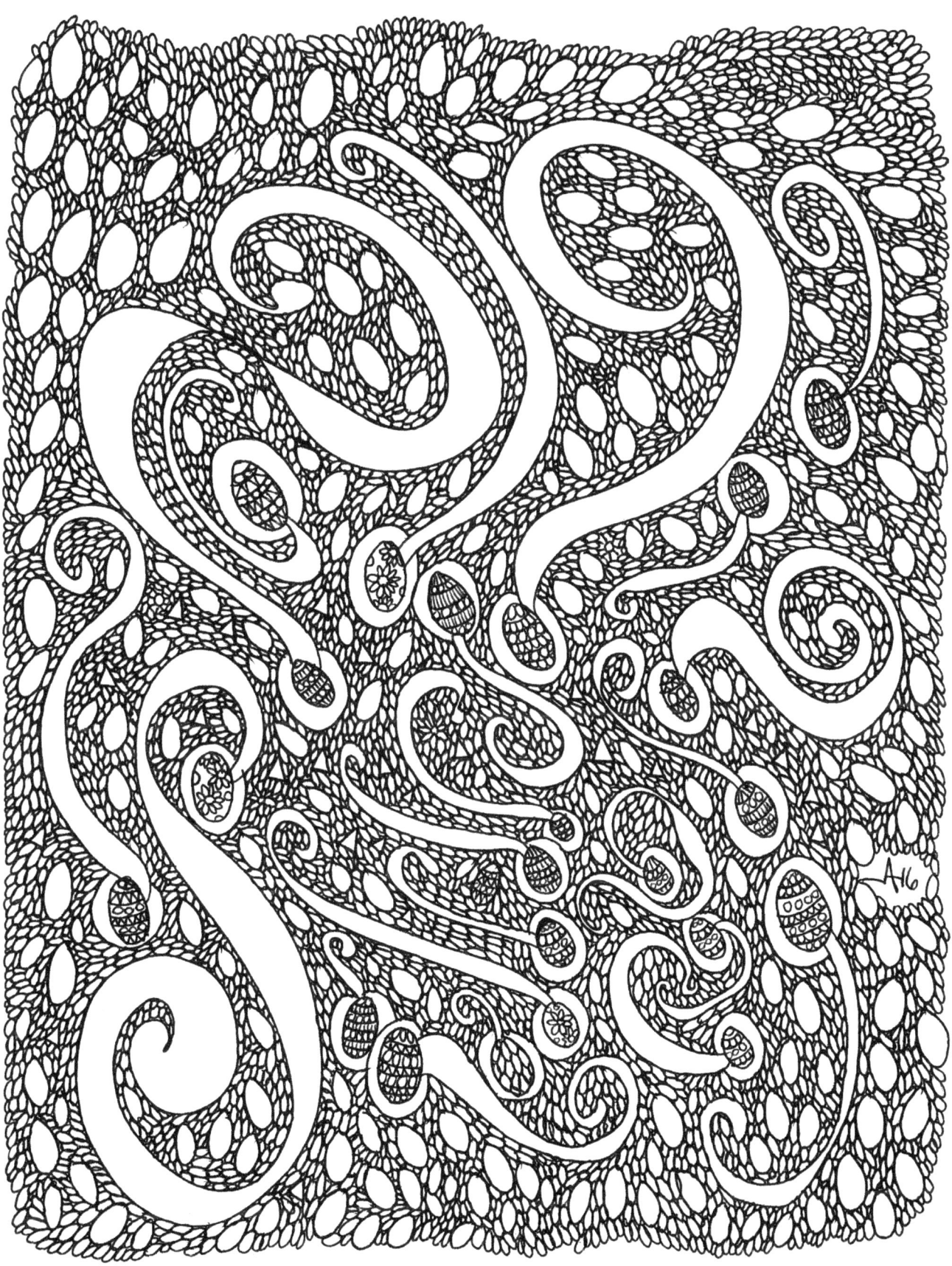

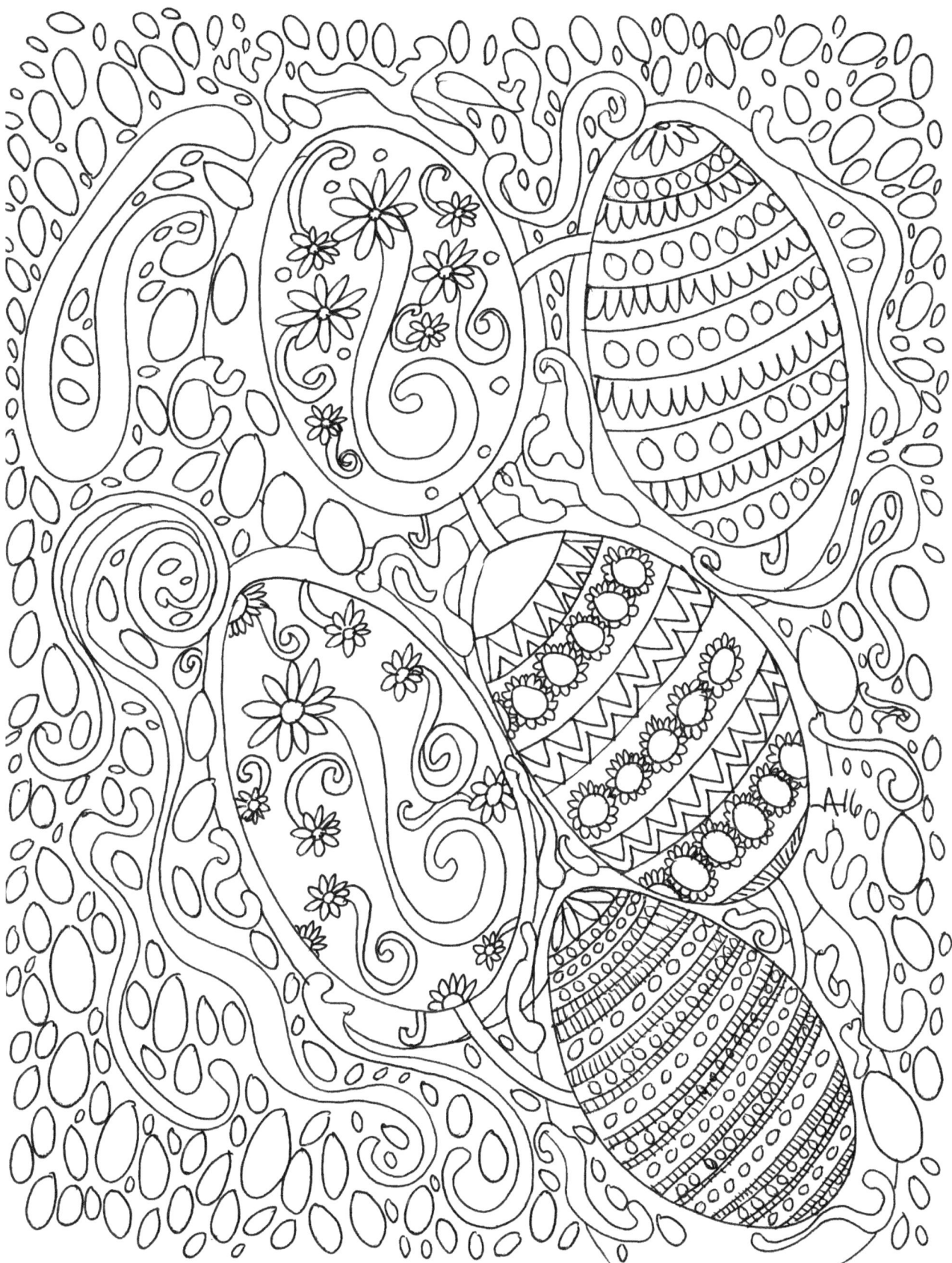

www.ingramcontent.com/pod-product-compliance
Lightning Source LLC
Chambersburg PA
CBHW080628190526
45169CB00009B/3319